THE
MAKER'S
DIET

SHOPPER'S GUIDE

JORDAN S. RUBIN

D0681553

Contents

Introduction

THE MAKER'S DIET 40-DAY HEALTH EXPERIENCE IS the complete program that has helped many thousands of people achieve total wellness. It arose out of my own health struggles—battling with Crohn's disease and finding little help from traditional medicine—and has grown into the full system as presented in *The Maker's Diet.*

This book, *The Maker's Diet Shopper's Guide,* is designed to be a practical tool for helping you and your family live out the three phases of the Maker's Diet. While the program includes spiritual life, physical fitness, and hygiene and purification, *The Maker's Diet Shopper's Guide* concentrates on nutrition.

To know how to eat on the Maker's Diet, you need to know what foods to prepare (Section 1: Meal Plans). To know what foods to prepare, you need to have recipes that work with the program (Section 2: Recipes). And to know how to prepare the recipes, you have to know what ingredients to purchase (Section 3: Shopping Lists).

It is my hope that *The Maker's Diet Shopper's Guide* gives you the nuts-and-bolts knowledge you need to succeed on the Maker's Diet 40-Day Health Experience.

Meal Plans

Your Daily Regimen

I HAVE DETAILED FOR YOU A DAILY REGIMEN FOR EACH phase of the protocol. And I have given you sample menus for every day of each two-week phase. (See *The Maker's Diet* for more information on this daily regimen and the terms I refer to.) In addition, you can always refer to Section 3: Shopping Lists to see the foods to enjoy for each phase and thus create your own healthy, delicious meals with a wide variety of natural, healing foods and beverages.

"Partial-fast" days

I have recommended a partial fast one day per week in each phase. (I recommend Thursday, as it is much more difficult to fast during the weekend.) On the partial-fast days you will not be eating breakfast or lunch. You should still consume your cleansing drink and other supplements. This partial-fast day allows the body to cleanse and rebuild. Make sure to consume lots of fluids during your partial-fast day, especially raw vegetable juices and pure water. To gain maximum spiritual benefit from your partial-fast days, I recommend praying each time you experience hunger.

Daily Regimen for Phase One: Days 1–14

Morning hygiene
Clenzology
Aromatherapy A.M.
Purification A.M.

Morning cleansing drink
Mix 2 tablespoons of a whole-food fiber blend and 1–2 tablespoons or 5 caplets of a green superfood blend with HSOs (optional for the hard-core dieter) in 8–12 ounces of purified water. Shake vigorously and drink immediately.

Morning tune-up
Morning prayer
Exercise (5–10 minutes): Choose one—Functional Fitness, rebounding, or breathing exercises. During exercise listen to music that is uplifting and energizing.

Breakfast
See sample breakfast menus for days 1–14.

Breakfast supplements
Living multivitamin/mineral with homeostatic nutrients, 2–3 caplets.

Lunch
See sample lunch menus for days 1–14.

Lunch supplements

Living multivitamin/mineral with homeostatic nutrients, 2–3 caplets.

Afternoon cleansing drink

Mix 2 tablespoons of a whole-food fiber blend and 1–2 tablespoons or 5 caplets of a green superfood blend with HSOs (optional for the hard-core dieter) in 8–12 ounces of purified water. Shake vigorously and drink immediately.

Dinner

See sample dinner menus for days 1–14.

Dinner supplements

Living multivitamin/mineral with homeostatic nutrients, 2–3 caplets.

Icelandic Cod Liver Oil: 1 teaspoon to 1 tablespoon based on sun exposure. If you receive more than two hours of direct sunlight per week, you may take 1–2 teaspoons. If you receive less than two hours of direct sunlight per week, you may take 1 tablespoon.

Evening snack

See sample snack menus for days 1–14.

Evening wind down

Evening prayer

Exercise (5–10 minutes): Choose one—Functional Fitness, rebounding, or breathing exercises. During exercise listen to music that is uplifting and energizing.

Evening hygiene
Clenzology
Aromatherapy P.M.
Purification P.M.

In bed before 10:30

Suggested Meal Plans for Phase One

Day 1

Breakfast
Fried eggs (prepared any way you desire: over-easy, medium, or well. Fry in extra-virgin coconut oil or butter.)
Stir-fried veggies

Lunch
Tuna Salad (page 59)
Raw carrots and celery

Dinner
French-style London Broil (page 69)
Green salad

Evening snack
½ cup strawberries
1 oz. raw goat's milk cheese

Day 2

Breakfast
Vegetable Frittata (page 55)

Lunch

Coconut Milk Soup (page 40)

Dinner

Wild Alaskan Salmon With Pecan Pesto (page 57)

Green salad

Cultured vegetables

Evening snack

Carrot, celery, and raw almond butter

Day 3

Breakfast

Onion, Pepper, and Goat Cheese Omelet (page 54)

Avocado slices with seasoning

Lunch

Oriental Red Meat Salad (page 43)

Dinner

Coconut Milk Soup (page 40), left over from day 2

Easy Broiled Halibut (page 56)

Green salad

Evening snack

Goat's milk yogurt

Raw honey, vanilla, and blueberries

Day 4

Breakfast

Easy Soft-boiled/Hardboiled Eggs (page 53)

Steamed broccoli with butter

Lunch

Coconut Milk Soup (page 40), left over from day 2

Dinner

Green salad

Wild Duck (page 64)

Evening snack

Raw soaked almonds

Raw milk cheese

Day 5

Breakfast

None (partial-fast day)

Lunch

None (partial-fast day)

Dinner

Cultured veggies

Green salad

Tuna Steaks, Oriental Style (page 59)

Evening snack

None (partial-fast day)

Day 6

Breakfast

Mushroom Swiss Omelet (page 54)

Lunch

Chicken Salad (page 60)

Dinner

Green salad

Steamed asparagus with butter
Easy Broiled Steak (page 66)

Evening snack

Raspberries
Raw milk cheese

Day 7

Breakfast

Fried eggs
Avocado
Salsa

Lunch

Beef Soup (page 37)

Dinner

Steamed vegetable medley
Chicken With Oregano and Mushrooms (page 60)

Evening snack

Probiogurt and a small amount of honey

Day 8

Breakfast

Tomato Basil Omelet (page 54)

Lunch

Tuna Tahini Salad (page 44)
Raw carrot, cucumber, and celery

Dinner

Beef Soup (page 37), left over from day 7

Easy Curried Chicken (page 61)
Steamed broccoli

Evening snack

½ cup blueberries
Probiogurt with ½ tsp. honey

Day 9

Breakfast

Vegetable Frittata (page 55)
"Live" salsa

Lunch

Beef Soup (page 37), left over from day 7

Dinner

Green salad
Chevon Meat Loaf (page 65), or other red meat loaf

Evening snack

Pepitas (page 78)

Day 10

Breakfast

Sausage and Pepper Omelet (page 54)

Lunch

Salmon Salad (page 57)
Carrot and celery sticks

Dinner

Chicken Fajitas (with no tortilla) over mixed greens
(page 62)

Evening snack

½ cup blackberries

1 oz. goat cheddar cheese

Day 11

Breakfast

Scrambled eggs with cheese

Lunch

Grilled chicken over mixed greens

Dinner

Red Meat Chili (page 41)

Green salad

Evening snack

Soaked almonds

Goat's milk cottage cheese

Day 12

Breakfast

None (partial-fast day)

Lunch

None (partial-fast day)

Dinner

Cultured veggies

Green salad

Easy Smothered Salmon (page 56)

Evening snack

None (partial-fast day)

Day 13

Breakfast

Naturally smoked salmon

Thinly sliced cheddar cheese

½ avocado filled with salsa

Lunch

Hamburger patty with grilled, roasted, or sautéed onions, peppers, and mushrooms

Green salad

Dinner

Roasted Pastured Chicken (page 63)

Roasted vegetables (peppers, onions, carrots, peas, broccoli)

Evening snack

Carrots, celery, and raw almond butter

Day 14

Breakfast

Spinach and Feta Omelet (page 54)

Lunch

Tuna Salad (page 59)

Dinner

Green salad

Easy Pepper Steak (page 68)

Evening snack

Mixed berries (strawberries, blueberries, raspberries, blackberries)

Goat's milk cottage cheese or cheddar cheese

Daily Regimen for Phase Two: Days 15–28

Morning hygiene
Clenzology
Hydrotherapy shower
Aromatherapy A.M.
Purification A.M.

Morning cleansing drink
Mix 2 tablespoons of a whole-food fiber blend and 1–2 tablespoons or 5 caplets of a green superfood blend with HSOs (optional for the hard-core dieter) in 8–12 ounces of purified water. Shake vigorously and drink immediately.

Morning tune-up
Morning prayer
Exercise (10–15 minutes): Choose one—Functional Fitness, rebounding, or breathing exercises. During exercise listen to music that is uplifting and energizing.

Breakfast
See sample breakfast menus for days 15–28.

Breakfast supplements
Living multivitamin/mineral with homeostatic nutrients, 2–3 caplets.

Lunch
See sample lunch menus for days 15–28.

Lunch supplements

Living multivitamin/mineral with homeostatic nutrients, 2–3 caplets.

Afternoon cleansing drink

Mix 2 tablespoons of a whole-food fiber blend and 1–2 tablespoons or 5 caplets of a green superfood blend with HSOs (optional for the hard-core dieter) in 8–12 ounces of purified water. Shake vigorously and drink immediately.

Dinner

See sample dinner menus for days 15–28.

Dinner supplements

Living multivitamin/mineral with homeostatic nutrients, 2–3 caplets.

Icelandic Cod Liver Oil: 1 teaspoon to 1 tablespoon based on sun exposure. If you receive more than two hours of direct sunlight per week, you may take 1–2 teaspoons. If you receive less than two hours of direct sunlight per week, you may take 1 tablespoon.

Evening snack

See sample snack menus for days 15–28.

Evening wind down

Evening prayer

Exercise (10–15 minutes): Choose one—Functional Fitness, rebounding, or breathing exercises. During exercise listen to music that is uplifting and energizing.

Evening hygiene
>   Clenzology
>   Aromatherapy P.M.
>   Purification P.M.
>   Healing bath (optional)

In bed before 10:30

Suggested Meal Plans for Phase Two

Day 15

Breakfast
>   Cottage cheese or ricotta cheese
>   Pineapple
>   Sliced almonds

Lunch
>   Uptown Salad (page 42)

Dinner
>   Venison Steaks With Marinade (page 70)
>   Sweet potatoes with butter
>   Steamed vegetable medley

Evening snack
>   Balanced Vegetable Juice (page 81)

Day 16

Breakfast
>   Garden Herb Omelet (page 54)
>   1 orange

Lunch

Salade Nicoise (page 44)

Dinner

Chicken With Oregano and Mushrooms (page 60)

Corn on the cob

Steamed broccoli and carrots with butter

Evening snack

Apple slices

Almond butter and honey

Day 17

Breakfast

Easy Soft-boiled/Hardboiled Eggs (page 53)

Avocado with salsa

Lunch

Chicken Soup/Stock (page 38)

Dinner

Red Snapper Mexican Style (page 58)

Black beans

Easy Vegetable Salad (page 42)

Evening snack

Mixed raw nuts (almonds, walnuts, pecans, Macadamia nuts)

Apple slices

1 oz. cheese

Day 18

Breakfast

>   Yogurt
>   Peaches
>   Raw honey

Lunch

>   Chicken Salad (page 60), with meat left over from Chicken Soup, day 17
>   Carrot and celery sticks

Dinner

>   Mushroom Soup (page 40), using chicken stock from day 17
>   Beef burger patty
>   Sautéed onions and peppers

Evening snack

>   Creamy High-Enzyme Dessert (page 87)

Day 19

Breakfast

>   None (partial-fast day)

Lunch

>   None (partial-fast day)

Dinner

>   Ginger Carrots (page 46)
>   Mushroom Soup (page 40)
>   Green salad
>   Grilled chicken breast
>   Pan-fried sweet potato in coconut oil or butter

Evening snack
>None (partial-fast day)

Day 20

Breakfast
>Garden Herb Omelet (page 54)
>Grapefruit

Lunch
>Salmon Salad (page 57)
>Carrot and celery sticks

Dinner
>Green salad
>Venison or lamb kabobs
>Grilled vegetables (peppers, onions, mushrooms)

Evening snack
>Balanced Vegetable Juice (page 81)

Day 21

Breakfast
>Fried eggs
>½ cup strawberries

Lunch
>Uptown Salad (with roast beef) (page 42)

Dinner
>Simple Baked Fish (page 56)
>Yogurt Tahini Inbetweeni (page 52)
>Steamed broccoli

Evening snack
>Sliced apples
>Nut or seed butter (almond, sesame, etc.)

Day 22

Breakfast
>Cottage cheese
>Honey
>Berries of choice

Lunch
>Tuna Tahini Salad (page 44)

Dinner
>Easy Curried Chicken (page 61)
>Zucchini and onions
>Baked sweet potato with butter

Evening snack
>Creamy High-Enzyme Dessert (page 87)

Day 23

Breakfast
>Sausage and Pepper Omelet (page 54)

Lunch
>Chicken Soup (page 38)
>Green salad

Dinner
>Wild Alaskan Salmon With Pecan Pesto (page 57)
>Steamed leeks and asparagus

Evening snack
> 1 oz. cheddar cheese
> ½ cup strawberries

Day 24

Breakfast
> Easy Soft-boiled/Hardboiled Eggs (page 53)
> ½ avocado with salsa or seasoning

Lunch
> Chicken Salad (page 60), using leftover chicken from Chicken Soup, day 23

Dinner
> Coconut Milk Soup (page 40), using leftover chicken stock from day 23
> Easy Smothered Salmon (page 56)
> Steamed broccoli, carrots, and peas

Evening snack
> Pear slices
> Almond butter

Day 25

Breakfast
> Yogurt or kefir
> Berries
> Almond slices

Lunch
> Coconut Milk Soup (page 40), using leftover chicken stock from day 23
> Green salad

Dinner

Easy Pepper Steak (page 68)

Marinated sautéed portabello mushrooms and onions

Evening snack

1 orange

Sunflower seeds

Day 26

Breakfast

None (partial-fast day)

Lunch

None (partial-fast day)

Dinner

Cultured vegetables

Green salad

Cilantro Lime Chicken Cacciatore (page 61)

Black beans

Evening snack

None (partial-fast day)

Day 27

Breakfast

Onion, Pepper, and Goat Cheese Omelet (page 54)

Lunch

Salmon Salad (page 57)

Dinner

Ginger Carrots (page 46)

Grilled or sautéed chicken or fish of choice

Steamed or sautéed vegetables of choice

Evening snack

Fruit salad with allowable fruits of your choice

Dollop of yogurt or cottage cheese

Day 28

Breakfast

Vegetable Frittata (page 55)

½ cup raspberries

Lunch

Oriental Red Meat Salad (page 43)

Dinner

Tuna Steaks, Oriental Style (page 59)

Mixed greens

Steamed asparagus

Sautéed mushrooms

Evening snack

Pepitas (page 78)

Daily Regimen for Phase Three: Days 29–40

Morning hygiene
Clenzology
Hydrotherapy shower and scrub
Aromatherapy A.M.
Purification A.M.

Morning cleansing drink
Mix 2 tablespoons of a whole-food fiber blend and 1–2 tablespoons or 5 caplets of a green superfood blend with HSOs (optional for the hard-core dieter) in 8–12 ounces of purified water. Shake vigorously and drink immediately.

Morning tune-up
Morning prayer
Exercise (15–20 minutes): Choose one—Functional Fitness, rebounding, or breathing exercises. During exercise listen to music that is uplifting and energizing.

Breakfast
See sample breakfast menus for days 29–40.

Breakfast supplements
Living multivitamin/mineral with homeostatic nutrients, 2–3 caplets.

Lunch
See sample lunch menus for days 29–40.

Lunch supplements

Living multivitamin/mineral with homeostatic nutrients, 2–3 caplets.

Afternoon cleansing drink (optional)

Mix 2 tablespoons of a whole-food fiber blend and 1–2 tablespoons or 5 caplets of a green superfood blend with HSOs (optional for the hard-core dieter) in 8–12 ounces of purified water. Shake vigorously and drink immediately.

Dinner

See sample dinner menus for days 29–40.

Dinner supplements

Living multivitamin/mineral with homeostatic nutrients, 2–3 caplets.

Icelandic Cod Liver Oil: 1 teaspoon to 1 tablespoon based on sun exposure. If you receive more than two hours of direct sunlight per week, you may take 1–2 teaspoons. If you receive less than two hours of direct sunlight per week, you may take 1 tablespoon.

Evening wind down

Evening prayer

Exercise (15–20 minutes): Choose one—Functional Fitness, rebounding, or breathing exercises. During exercise listen to music that is uplifting and energizing.

Evening hygiene

Clenzology

Aromatherapy P.M.
Purification P.M.
Healing bath (optional)

In bed before 10:30

Suggested Meal Plans for Phase Three

Day 29

Breakfast

Berry Smoothie (page 84)

Lunch

Sliced turkey and avocado sandwich on toasted sprouted or whole-grain sourdough bread

Carrot and celery sticks

Dinner

Barbecue-style chicken breast
Pan-roasted red bliss potatoes
Steamed asparagus

Day 30

Breakfast

Tomato Basil Omelet (page 54)
1 orange or grapefruit

Lunch

Uptown Salad (page 42)

Dinner

Lamb Chops (page 66)
Baked potato with butter

Steamed vegetables (carrots, peas, broccoli)

Day 31

Breakfast

Fried eggs

Blueberry Pecan Pancakes (page 78)

Lunch

Green salad

Chicken Soup (page 38)

Dinner

Green salad

Easy Broiled Halibut (page 56)

Steamed broccoli

Day 32

Breakfast

Cottage cheese

Tropical fruit (mango, papaya, banana, pineapple)

Raw honey

Lunch

Chicken Salad (page 60), with leftover chicken from soup on day 31

Carrot and celery sticks

Dinner

Cultured vegetables

Beef Soup (page 37)

Grilled salmon teriyaki

Brown rice

Day 33

Breakfast

None (partial-fast day)

Lunch

None (partial-fast day)

Dinner

Raw Sauerkraut (page 47)

Green salad

Beef Soup (page 37)

Chicken Fajitas (page 62)

Sprouted tortillas

Salsa, guacamole, sour cream

Day 34

Breakfast

Pina Colada Smoothie (page 85)

Lunch

Tuna Tahini Salad (page 44)

Dinner

Green salad

Spicy Chicken Stuffed Peppers (page 62)

Day 35

Breakfast

Spinach and Feta Omelet (page 54)

½ cup berries of choice

Lunch

Roast beef sandwich on sprouted or sourdough

whole-grain bread
Carrot and celery sticks

Dinner
Simple Baked Fish (page 56)
Steamed vegetables
Baked sweet potato

Day 36

Breakfast
Cottage cheese or yogurt
Fruit of choice

Lunch
Salmon Salad (page 57)
Apple slices

Dinner
Easy Curried Chicken (page 61)
Couscous (bulgur wheat)
Stir-fried broccoli, onions, mushrooms

Day 37

Breakfast
Oatmeal
Raisins
Sliced almonds

Lunch
Grilled chicken
Green salad

Dinner
> Green salad
> French-style London Broil (page 69)
> Roasted new potatoes

Day 38

Breakfast
> Mushroom Swiss Omelet (page 54)

Lunch
> Uptown Salad (with turkey breast) (page 42)

Dinner
> Green salad
> Quinoa with onions and peas
> Broiled grouper with citrus marinade

Day 39

Breakfast
> Peaches 'n Cream Smoothie (page 85)

Lunch
> Red Meat Chili (page 41)

Dinner
> Green salad
> Easy Broiled Steak (page 66)
> Baked potato

Day 40

Breakfast
> Easy Whole-Grain Waffles (page 75)

Lunch

    Salade Nicoise (page 44)

Dinner

    Green salad

    Chicken With Oregano and Mushrooms (page 60)

    Steamed vegetables

Section 2

Recipes

Soups and Stocks

BEEF SOUP/STOCK

About 6 lb. beef marrow and knuckle bones	3 celery stalks, coarsely chopped
1 calf's foot, cut into pieces (optional)	Several sprigs of fresh thyme, tied together
5 lb. meaty rib or neck bones	1 tsp. dried green peppercorns, crushed
4 or more quarts cold, filtered water	1 bunch parsley
3 onions, coarsely chopped	¼ cup vinegar
3 carrots, coarsely chopped	

Good beef stock must be made with several sorts of beef bones. Knuckle bones and feet impart large quantities of gelatin to the broth; marrow bones impart flavor and the particular nutrients of the bone marrow; and meaty rib or neck bones add color and flavor.

Place the knuckle and marrow bones and calf's foot (optional) in a very large pot; cover with water. Let stand for one hour. Meanwhile, place meaty bones in a roasting pan and brown at 350 degrees in the oven. When well browned, add to the pot along with vinegar and vegetables.

Pour fat from roasting pan, add cold water, set over a high flame, and bring to a boil, stirring with a wooden spoon to de-glaze. Add this liquid to the pot. Add additional water, if necessary, to cover the bones, but the liquid should come no higher than within 1 inch of the rim of the pot, as the volume expands slightly during cooking. Bring to a boil. A large amount of scum will come to the top. It is important to remove this with a spoon. After you have skimmed, reduce heat and add the thyme and crushed peppercorns.

Simmer stock for at least 12 hours and for as long as 72 hours. Just before finishing, add the parsley. Let it wilt and remove stock from heat.

You will now have a pot of rather repulsive-looking brown liquid containing globs of gelatinous and fatty material. It doesn't even smell particularly good. But don't despair. After straining, you will have a delicious and nourishing clear broth that forms the basis for many other recipes in this book.

Remove bones with tongs or a slotted spoon. Strain the stock into a large bowl. Let cool in the refrigerator, and remove the congealed fat that rises to the top. Reheat and transfer to storage containers.

Note: Your dog will love the leftover meat and bones.

VARIATION: LAMB STOCK

Use lamb bones, especially lamb neck bones. This makes a delicious stock.

From *Nourishing Traditions* by Sally Fallon. Used by permission.

CHICKEN SOUP/STOCK

1 whole chicken (free range, pastured or organic)	6 celery stalks, coarsely chopped
	2–4 zucchinis
2–4 chicken feet (optional)	4–6 Tbsp. extra-virgin coconut oil
3–4 quarts cold-filtered water	1 bunch parsley
1 Tbsp. raw apple cider vinegar	5 garlic cloves
4 medium-sized onions, coarsely chopped	4 inches grated ginger
	2–4 Tbsp. Celtic salt
8 carrots, peeled and coarsely chopped	

If you are using a whole chicken, remove fat glands and gizzards from the cavity. By all means, use chicken feet if you can find them—they are full of gelatin. (Jewish folklore considers the addition of chicken feet the secret to successful broth.) Place chicken or chicken pieces in a large stainless steel pot with the water, vinegar, and all vegetables except parsley. Bring to a boil, and remove scum that rises to the top. Cover and cook on low heat for 12 to 24 hours.

The longer you cook the stock, the richer and more flavorful it will be. About five minutes before finishing the stock, add parsley. This will impart additional mineral ions to the broth.

Remove from heat, and take chicken out of pot. Let it cool, then remove meat from the carcass. Reserve for other uses such as chicken salads, enchiladas, sandwiches, or curries. (The skin and smaller bones, which will be very soft, may be given to your dog or cat.) Strain the stock into a large bowl and reserve in your refrigerator for use as a base for other soups.

VARIATIONS: TURKEY STOCK AND DUCK STOCK

Prepare as chicken stock using turkey wings and drumsticks or duck carcasses from which the breasts, legs, and thighs have been removed. These stocks will have a stronger flavor than chicken stock and will profit from the addition of several sprigs of fresh thyme tied together during cooking.

From *Nourishing Traditions* by Sally Fallon. Used by permission.

FISH STOCK

3 or 4 whole carcasses, including heads, of non-oily fish such as sole, turbot, rockfish, or snapper	Several sprigs fresh thyme Several sprigs parsley 1 bay leaf
2 Tbsp. extra-virgin coconut oil or butter	½ cup dry white wine or vermouth 1 Tbsp. apple cider vinegar
2 onions, coarsely chopped	
1 carrot, coarsely chopped	

Melt coconut oil or butter in a large stainless steel pot. Add the vegetables and cook very gently, about 30 minutes, until they are soft. Add wine and bring to a boil. Add fish carcasses and cover with cold, filtered water. Add vinegar. Bring to a boil. Take the time to carefully skim off the scum and impurities as they rise to the top. Tie herbs together and add to the pot. Reduce heat; cover and simmer for at least 4 hours or overnight. Remove carcasses with tongs or a slotted spoon, and strain the liquid into pint-sized storage containers for refrigerator or freezer.

The carrot will add a delicate sweetness to the stock when it has been reduced. Do not be tempted to add more carrots to the stock, or your final sauce will be too sweet!

From *Nourishing Traditions* by Sally Fallon. Used by permission.

COCONUT MILK SOUP

1½ quarts homemade fish or chicken stock	1 Tbsp. grated fresh ginger
1½ cups coconut milk and cream	2 Tbsp. fish sauce (optional)
1 lb. chicken or fish, cut into small cubes	2–4 Tbsp. lime juice
3 jalapeño chilies, diced, or ½ tsp. cayenne pepper, dried	Chopped cilantro for garnish

Simmer all ingredients until meat is cooked through. Garnish with cilantro. **Serves 6–8.**

From *Nourishing Traditions* by Sally Fallon. Used by permission.

MUSHROOM SOUP

2 medium onions, peeled and chopped	1 piece toasted whole-grain sprouted or sourdough bread, broken into pieces
3 Tbsp. extra-virgin coconut oil or butter	Freshly ground nutmeg
2 lb. fresh mushrooms	Sea salt or fish sauce and pepper to taste
Butter and extra-virgin olive oil	Sour cream or creme fraiche
1 quart chicken stock	
½ cup dry white wine	

The mushrooms must be very fresh! Sauté the onions gently in extra-virgin coconut oil or butter until soft. Meanwhile, wash mushrooms (no need to remove stems) and dry well. Cut into quarters. In a heavy cast-iron skillet, sauté the mushrooms in small batches in a mixture of butter and olive oil. Remove with slotted spoon and drain on paper towels. Add sautéed mushrooms, wine, bread, and chicken stock to onions; bring to a boil, and then skim. Reduce heat and simmer about 15 minutes.

Blend soup with a handheld blender. Add nutmeg and season to taste. Ladle into heated soup bowls and serve with cultured cream. **Serves 6.**

From *Nourishing Traditions* by Sally Fallon. Used by permission.

RED MEAT CHILI

3 lb. coarsely ground beef, buffalo, or game
Extra-virgin olive oil
¼ cup red wine
2 cups homemade beef stock
2 onions, finely chopped
2–4 small green chilies, hot or mild, seeded and chopped
2 cans tomatoes, briefly chopped in food processor
3 cloves garlic, peeled and mashed

1 Tbsp. ground cumin
2 Tbsp. dried oregano
2 Tbsp. dried basil
¼ to ½ tsp. red chili flakes
4 cups cooked, soaked kidney beans
No-oil chips for garnish
Chopped green onions for garnish
Creme fraiche or sour cream for garnish
Avocado slices for garnish
Chopped cilantro for garnish

Brown meat until crumbly in a little olive oil in a heavy pot. (Olive oil may not be necessary if the beef contains a lot of fat.) Add remaining ingredients. Simmer about 1 hour. Serve with garnishes. **SERVES 8–12.**

From *Nourishing Traditions* by Sally Fallon. Used by permission.

EASY VEGETABLE SALAD

1 head romaine, Boston, or red lettuce (or mixed greens)	• 2 plum tomatoes, seeded and chopped
	• ½ red onion, sliced
½ zucchini, quartered	• 2–3 oz. raw cheddar cheese, grated
½ cucumber, quartered	• Dressing of your choice

Place enough lettuce to cover the bottom of your salad bowl, then add a layer each of the other items, then another layer of lettuce, repeating until all ingredients are used up. Serve the dressing on the side, or mix into the entire salad and serve.
SERVES 4.

From *The Lazy Person's Whole Food Cookbook* by Stephen Byrnes. Used by permission.

UPTOWN SALAD

Romaine, Boston, red lettuce, or mixed greens	• 1 tomato, sliced
	• ½ red onion, sliced
4 oz. turkey breast or roast beef	• ½ avocado, sliced
½ red pepper	• 2–3 oz. Gorgonzola cheese, grated
½ cucumber, quartered	• Dressing of your choice

SERVES 1.

By Brian Upton. Used by permission.

ITALIAN SALAD

1 head romaine	1 small red onion, finely sliced
1 bunch watercress	½ cup small seed sprouts
1 red pepper, seeded and cut into a julienne	2 carrots, peeled and grated
	1 cup red cabbage, finely shredded
1 cucumber, peeled, seeded, quartered lengthwise, and finely sliced	1 cup cooked chickpeas
	¾ cup Basic Salad Dressing (page 48) or garlic dressing
1 heart of celery with leaves, finely chopped	

This is a good, basic salad. Children love it. The secret is to cut everything up small. Remove the outer leaves of the romaine, slice off the end, and open up to rinse out any dirt or impurities, while keeping the head intact. Pat dry. Slice across at ½-inch intervals. Place romaine in your salad bowl, then watercress, then add chopped vegetables in different piles. Finally strew sprouts and garbanzo beans over the top for an attractive presentation. Bring to the table to show off your creation before tossing with dressing. May be served with grated Parmesan cheese. **SERVES 6.**

VARIATION: MEXICAN SALAD

Use Mexican dressing rather than Basic Salad Dressing or garlic dressing. Omit chickpeas. Top with a sprinkle of pepitas, or thin strips of sprouted wheat tortillas, sautéed in olive oil until crisp.

From *Nourishing Traditions* by Sally Fallon. Used by permission.

ORIENTAL RED MEAT SALAD

1½ lb. beef flank steak, or similar cut from lamb or game	1 tsp. grated fresh ginger
	Pinch of red pepper flakes
½ cup lemon juice	2 Tbsp. toasted sesame seeds
6 Tbsp. soy sauce	½ lb. snow peas, steamed lightly and cut into quarters at an angle
2 Tbsp. extra-virgin olive oil or expeller-expressed peanut oil	
	1 pound bean sprouts, steamed lightly
1 Tbsp. toasted sesame oil	1 red pepper, seeded and cut into a julienne

Using a sharp knife, score the flank steak or red meat pieces across the grain on both sides. Broil 3 or 4 minutes to a side, or until meat is medium rare. Transfer to a cutting board and let stand for 10 minutes. Meanwhile, mix lemon juice, soy sauce, oils, ginger, and red pepper flakes together. Cut the meat across the grain on an angle into very thin slices, then cut these slices into a julienne. Marinate with soy sauce mixture for several hours in refrigerator. Mix with sesame seeds and vegetables just before serving. **Serves 6.**

From *Nourishing Traditions* by Sally Fallon. Used by permission.

SALADE NICOISE

6 portions fresh tuna steak, about 4 ounces each	1 lb. French beans, blanched for 8 minutes and rinsed under cold water
Extra-virgin olive oil	2 dozen small black olives
6 cups baby salad greens or frise lettuce	2 cups herb dressing, made with finely chopped parsley
6 small ripe tomatoes, cut into wedges	
6 small red potatoes, cooked in a clay pot	

Brush tuna steaks with olive oil, and season with sea salt and pepper. Using a heavy skillet, cook rapidly, two at a time, for about 4 minutes per side. Set aside.

Divide salad greens between 6 large plates. Garnish with tomatoes, potatoes, beans, and olives. Place steaks on top of greens. Add dressing. This is delicious with sourdough bread or pizza toasts. **Serves 6.**

From *Nourishing Traditions* by Sally Fallon. Used by permission.

TUNA TAHINI SALAD

2 large cans water-packed tuna, drained and flaked	Melted butter and extra-virgin olive oil
¼ tsp. cayenne pepper	⅓ cup toasted pine nuts
2 cups tahini sauce (see below)	Cilantro sprigs for garnish
4 medium onions, thinly sliced	Toasted, sprouted, or sourdough bread or sprouted crackers

Mix tuna with cayenne pepper and 1 cup sauce. Meanwhile, strew the onions on an oiled cookie sheet; brush with mixture of melted butter and olive oil, and bake at 375 degrees until crisp. Mound tuna on a platter. Scatter onions and pine nuts on top. Garnish with cilantro, and serve with dehydrated, sprouted, whole-grain crackers and remaining sauce. **SERVES 6–8.**

From *Nourishing Traditions* by Sally Fallon. Used by permission.

TAHINI SAUCE

2 cloves garlic, peeled and coarsely chopped	1 Tbsp. unrefined flaxseed oil
1 tsp. sea salt	1 cup water
½ cup tahini	½ cup fresh lemon juice

Place garlic in food processor with salt. Blend until minced. Add tahini and flaxseed oil and blend. Using attachment that allows addition of liquids drop by drop and with motor running, add water. When completely blended, add lemon juice all at once and blend until smooth. Sauce should be the consistency of heavy cream. If too thick, add more water and lemon juice. **MAKES 2 CUPS.**

From *Nourishing Traditions* by Sally Fallon. Used by permission.

Vegetables

General preparation guidelines: Do not boil vegetables unless this is required to eat them. Steam your veggies for a few minutes, then add butter or ghee, seasonings, and serve. You can also sauté your vegetables in extra-virgin coconut oil. Raw veggies with a healthy dressing or dip are also good.

EASY SAUTÉED GREENS

1 quart spinach or other greens	Sea salt/pepper to taste
Extra-virgin coconut oil	

Wash the spinach or greens in several waters. Remove all stems and brown leaves. Heat extra-virgin coconut oil in skillet. Place leaves in the skillet and cover. Cook till wilted, stirring occasionally. Season as you like. **SERVES 6–8.**

From *The Lazy Person's Whole Food Cookbook* by Stephen Byrnes. Used by permission.

Cultured Vegetables

GINGER CARROTS

4 cups grated carrots, loosely packed	2 Tbsp. whey (if not available, add an
1 Tbsp. fresh ginger, grated	additional 1 tsp. salt)
2 tsp. sea salt	

This is the best introduction to lacto-fermented vegetables we know. The taste is delicious, and the sweetness of the carrots neutralizes the acidity that some people find disagreeable when first introduced to lacto-fermented vegetables. Ginger carrots go well with fish and with highly spiced meats.

In a bowl, mix all ingredients and pound with wooden pounder to release juices. Place in a quart-sized, wide-mouth Mason jar and press down with the wooden pounder. There should be about an inch of space between the top of carrots and the top of the jar. Cover tightly. Leave at room temperature about 2–3 days before transferring to cold storage. **MAKES 1 QUART.**

From *Nourishing Traditions* by Sally Fallon. Used by permission.

RAW SAUERKRAUT

4 cups shredded cabbage, loosely packed	• 2 tsp. Celtic sea salt
½ tsp. cumin seeds	• 2 Tbsp. homemade whey
½ tsp. mustard seeds	• 1 cup filtered water

In a bowl, mix cabbage with cumin and mustard seeds. Mash or pound with a wooden pounder for several minutes to release juices. Place in a quart-sized, wide-mouthed Mason jar and pack down with the pounder. Mix water with sea salt and whey, and pour into jar. Add more water if needed to bring liquid to top of cabbage. There should be about one inch of space between the top of cabbage and the top of the jar. Cover tightly, and keep at room temperature for about 3 days. Transfer to cold storage. The sauerkraut can be eaten immediately, but it improves with age. **MAKES 1 QUART.**

From *Nourishing Traditions* by Sally Fallon. Used by permission.

Sauces, Dressings, Dips

BASIC SALAD DRESSING

½ cup extra-virgin olive oil
1 Tbsp. unrefined flaxseed oil
2 Tbsp. apple cider vinegar or lemon
  juice

- 1 tsp. Dijon-type mustard
- Herbamare seasoning to taste

Combine all ingredients and blend slowly. **MAKES ABOUT ¾ CUP.**

Adapted from *Nourishing Traditions* by Sally Fallon. Used by permission.

BALSAMIC DRESSING

1 tsp. Dijon-type dressing, smooth or
  grainy
2 Tbsp. plus 1 tsp. balsamic vinegar

- ½ cup extra-virgin olive oil
- 1 Tbsp. unrefined flaxseed oil

Balsamic vinegar is a red wine vinegar that has been aged in wooden casks. It has a delicious, pungent flavor that goes well with dark greens such as watercress or mache. Prepare as in Basic Salad Dressing recipe. **MAKES ABOUT ¾ CUP.**

From *Nourishing Traditions* by Sally Fallon. Used by permission.

BARBECUE SAUCE

¾ cup teriyaki sauce

- ¾ cup naturally sweetened ketchup

Mix ketchup into teriyaki sauce with a whisk. **MAKES 1½ CUPS.**

From *Nourishing Traditions* by Sally Fallon. Used by permission.

BETTER BUTTER

½ cup raw or organic butter (unsalted)
½ cup extra-virgin coconut oil

- ½ cup flaxseed or hempseed oil
- ¼ tsp. fine Celtic sea salt

Allow butter and coconut oil to soften at room temperature. Combine with flaxseed or hempseed oil, and add salt. Refrigerate and use as a spread. Note: Never use

Better Butter for cooking. The essential fatty acids contained in the oil will be damaged by the heat. **MAKES 1½ CUPS.**

By Jordan Rubin

CREAMY AVOCADO DIP

1 ripe avocado, peeled and cut into pieces	• Juice of 1 lemon
3 anchovy fillets (optional)	• 2 tsp. unrefined flaxseed oil
½ cup sour cream or creme fraiche	• 1 clove garlic, mashed

Place all ingredients in food processor and blend until smooth. Chill well before serving. Serve with vegetable sticks or baked tortillas, broken into chips. **MAKES 1½ CUPS.**

From *Nourishing Traditions* by Sally Fallon. Used by permission.

CREAMY DRESSING

¾ cup Basic Salad Dressing (page 48)	• ¼ cup sour cream, yogurt, or kefir

This is a traditional recipe of the Auvergne region of France. Prepare Basic Salad Dressing. Blend in cream with a fork. **MAKES ABOUT 1 CUP.**

From *Nourishing Traditions* by Sally Fallon. Used by permission.

EASY AVOCADO DRESSING

1 ripe avocado	• 2 Tbsp. extra-virgin olive oil
1 stalk of celery	• Herbamare seasoning to taste
1 small red pepper, seeded	

Blend avocado together with oil, celery, and pepper slices in blender until smooth.

From *The Lazy Person's Whole Food Cookbook* by Stephen Byrnes. Used by permission.

EASY FRENCH DRESSING

½ cup high-oleic safflower, sunflower, or walnut oil	¼ tsp. Herbamare seasoning
	¼ tsp. paprika
4 Tbsp. raw apple cider vinegar or lemon juice	Few grains of cayenne pepper
2 tsp. raw, unheated honey	

Combine dry ingredients and apple cider vinegar or lemon juice. Add oil slowly, beating constantly until thick.

From *The Lazy Person's Whole Food Cookbook* by Stephen Byrnes. Used by permission.

GUACAMOLE

2 ripe avocados	2 Tbsp. cilantro, finely chopped (optional)
Juice of 1 lemon	Pinch Celtic sea salt or Herbamare

Peel avocados. Place flesh in a bowl and squeeze lemon juice over it. Use a fork to mash (do not use a food processor). Guacamole should be slightly lumpy. Stir in the cilantro. Guacamole should be made just before serving as it will turn dark in an hour or two. Serve with vegetable sticks or baked tortillas, broken into chips. **MAKES 1½ CUPS.**

From *Nourishing Traditions* by Sally Fallon. Used by permission.

HERB DRESSING

¾ cup Basic Salad Dressing (page 48)	1 tsp. very finely chopped fresh herbs such as parsley, tarragon, thyme, basil, or oregano

Prepare Basic Salad Dressing and stir in herbs. **MAKES ABOUT ¾ CUP.**

From *Nourishing Traditions* by Sally Fallon. Used by permission.

ORIENTAL DRESSING

2 Tbsp. rice vinegar
1 Tbsp. soy sauce
1 tsp. grated ginger
1 tsp. toasted sesame oil
1 tsp. finely chopped green onion or
   chives

- 1 clove garlic, peeled and mashed
  (optional)
- ½ tsp. raw honey
- ½ cup extra-virgin olive oil
- 1 tsp. unrefined flaxseed oil

Place all ingredients in a jar and shake vigorously. **MAKES ABOUT ½ CUP.**
From *Nourishing Traditions* by Sally Fallon. Used by permission.

SALSA

4 medium tomatoes, peeled, seeded,
   and diced
2 small onions, finely diced
¼ cup diced chili pepper, hot or mild
1 bunch cilantro, chopped
1 tsp. dried oregano

- Juice of 2 lemons
- 2 tsp. Celtic sea salt
- 2 Tbsp. whey (if not available, use an
  additional 1 tsp. salt)
- ½–1 cup filtered water

Mix all ingredients except water, and place in a quart-sized, wide-mouth Mason jar.
Press down lightly with a wooden pounder. Add enough water to cover vegetables.
Cover tightly and keep at room temperature for 2 days before transferring to cold
storage. **MAKES 1 QUART.**
From *Nourishing Traditions* by Sally Fallon. Used by permission.

TERIYAKI SAUCE

1 Tbsp. grated fresh ginger
3 garlic cloves, mashed
1 Tbsp. toasted sesame oil

- 1 Tbsp. rice vinegar
- 1 Tbsp. raw honey
- ½ cup soy sauce

Use as a marinade for chicken or duck. Mix all ingredients together with a whisk.
MAKES ¾ CUP.
From *Nourishing Traditions* by Sally Fallon. Used by permission.

YOGURT TAHINI INBETWEENI

4 oz. Probiogurt
1 Tbsp. Dijon-style mustard
1 Tbsp. yellow or brown mustard

- Juice of one freshly squeezed lemon
- 1 Tbsp. raw tahini (sesame butter)
- ½ tsp. of fine Celtic sea salt

Combine all ingredients together and mix thoroughly.

By Jason Dewberry. Used by permission.

Eggs

EASY SCRAMBLED EGGS

6 eggs	• 3 Tbsp. melted butter or extra virgin
Celtic sea salt, pepper	• coconut oil
¼ cup heavy cream	• Few grains of cayenne pepper
	• (optional)

Beat eggs well. Add cream. Heat butter in skillet or pan; add egg mixture, cooking slowly, until of a creamy texture. If desired, 1 cup of chopped turkey bacon, chicken, beef, or peppers may be added for variations in taste. **SERVES 3–4.**

From *The Lazy Person's Whole Food Cookbook* by Stephen Byrnes. Used by permission.

EASY SOFT-BOILED/HARDBOILED EGGS

Wash eggs and cover with boiling water. Simmer for 4 minutes if you're making soft-boiled eggs, and 12 minutes if you're making hardboiled eggs. Hardboiled eggs may be plunged into cold water if you will be using them in another recipe, such as sliced additions or garnishes. Hardboiled eggs may also be made several at a time and then refrigerated for convenient snacking later.

From *The Lazy Person's Whole Food Cookbook* by Stephen Byrnes. Used by permission.

BASIC OMELET

4 fresh eggs, at room temperature	• Pinch sea salt
3 Tbsp. extra-virgin coconut oil or	•
butter	•
	•

Crack eggs into a bowl. Add water and sea salt, and blend with a wire whisk. (Do not over-whisk or the omelet will be tough). Melt coconut oil or butter in a well-seasoned cast iron skillet or frying pan. When foam subsides, add egg mixture. Tip pan to allow egg to cover the entire pan. Cook several minutes over medium heat until underside is lightly browned. Lift up one side with a spatula and fold omelet in half. Reduce heat and cook another 30 seconds or so—this will allow the egg on the inside to cook. Slide omelet onto a heated platter and serve. **SERVES 2.**

VARIATION: ONION, PEPPER, AND GOAT CHEESE OMELET

Sauté 1 small onion, thinly sliced, and ½ red pepper, cut into julienne strips, in a little extra-virgin coconut oil or butter until tender. Strew this evenly over the egg mixture as it begins to cook, along with 2 ounces of goat's milk cheddar or feta cheese.

VARIATION: GARDEN HERB OMELET

Scatter 1 tablespoon parsley, finely chopped, 1 tablespoon chives, finely chopped, and 1 tablespoon thyme or other garden herb, finely chopped, over omelet as it begins to cook.

VARIATION: MUSHROOM SWISS OMELET

Sauté ½ pound fresh mushrooms, washed, well dried, and thinly sliced, in extra-virgin coconut oil or butter and olive oil. Scatter mushrooms and grated Swiss cheese over the omelet as it begins to cook.

VARIATION: SAUSAGE AND PEPPER OMELET

Sauté ¼ cup turkey or buffalo sausage and red or yellow peppers in a little extra-virgin coconut oil or butter until crumbly. Scatter over the omelet as it begins to cook.

VARIATION: SPINACH AND FETA OMELET

Add chopped onion to beaten eggs. Add more onions, spinach, tomatoes, and feta cheese as it begins to cook.

VARIATION: TOMATO BASIL OMELET

Scatter ¼ cup diced tomato and chopped fresh basil over omelet as it begins to cook.

From *Nourishing Traditions* by Sally Fallon. Used by permission.

VEGETABLE FRITTATA

1 cup broccoli flowerets, steamed until tender and broken into small pieces	⅓ cup sour cream or creme fraiche
1 red pepper; seeded and cut into a julienne	1 tsp. finely grated lemon rind
	Pinch dried oregano
1 medium onion, peeled and finely chopped	Pinch dried rosemary
Butter and extra-virgin olive oil	Sea salt and freshly ground pepper
6 eggs	1 cup grated raw Monterey Jack cheese

In a cast iron skillet, sauté the pepper and onion in butter and olive oil until soft. Remove with a slotted spoon. Beat eggs with cream and seasonings. Stir in broccoli, peppers, and onion. Melt more butter and olive oil in the pan and pour in egg mixture. Cook over medium heat about 5 minutes until underside is golden. Sprinkle cheese on top and place under the broiler for a few minutes until the frittata puffs and browns. Cut into wedges and serve. **SERVES 4.**

From *Nourishing Traditions* by Sally Fallon. Used by permission. For variations of this recipe, order a copy of *Nourishing Traditions.*

SIMPLE BAKED FISH

1½ lb. filet of white fish such as sole, whiting, or turbot	• 1 Tbsp. fish sauce (optional)
	• Dash cayenne pepper
Juice of 1 lemon	• 1 Tbsp. snipped fresh herbs

Place fish in buttered baking dish. Sprinkle with lemon juice, cayenne, fish sauce, herbs, and salt. Cover baking dish with foil (but don't let foil touch the fish). Bake at 300 degrees for about 15 minutes. **SERVES 4.**

From *Nourishing Traditions* by Sally Fallon. Used by permission.

EASY BROILED HALIBUT

1–2 lb. halibut	• Sea salt or Herbamare
Lemon juice	• Pepper
Butter or extra-virgin coconut oil	

Wipe halibut slices with damp cloth and sprinkle with salt, pepper, and lemon juice. Dot with oil or butter. Broil under high heat, turning frequently till brown. **SERVES 6–8.**

From *The Lazy Person's Whole Food Cookbook* by Stephen Byrnes. Used by permission.

EASY SMOTHERED SALMON

2 cups canned salmon	• 2 Tbsp. melted extra-virgin coconut oil or butter
¾ cup diced celery	
2 slices turkey bacon, chopped	• ¾ cup onion, chopped
½ cup boiling water	• 1 tsp. sea salt
	• 2 thin slices lemon (optional)

Combine oil or butter, turkey bacon, celery, onion, and salt; fry until light brown. Place salmon in center of greased baking pan. Arrange vegetables and turkey bacon around salmon. Add water and cover. Bake at 375 degrees for 30 minutes. Remove cover and cook another 10 minutes. **SERVES 6.**

From T*he Lazy Person's Whole Food Cookbook* by Stephen Byrnes. Used by permission. For more salmon recipes, order a copy of this cookbook.

SALMON SALAD

1 can water-packed salmon	• Chopped onions
1 Tbsp. omega-3 mayonnaise	• Chopped peppers
1 Tbsp. flaxseed oil or garlic-chili flax	• Chopped celery

Combine all ingredients and serve over lettuce or toasted sprouted bread. **SERVES 1–2.**

By Jordan Rubin

WILD ALASKAN SALMON WITH PECAN PESTO

4 wild Alaskan salmon fillets (about 1.25–1.5 lb.)	• 1 3-inch sprig of rosemary
1/3 lb. shelled pecans	• Olive oil
3 oz. butter, cold	• Celtic sea salt
2–3 fresh jalapeños	• Pepper
1 small lemon or orange	

Heat oven to 300 degrees and toast pecans on a cookie sheet until you can smell the aroma of toasted pecans, about 20-30 minutes. Transfer to a cool cookie sheet. Rinse salmon and pat dry. Butterfly fillets with a sharp knife if desired. Rub salmon with olive oil; salt and pepper both sides. Heat iron skillet or other heavy skillet over medium heat. Sauté fillets until firm to the touch.

Prepare jalapeños by removing the tops and splitting lengthwise. De-rib and remove the seeds with a sharp knife. Chop coarsely. Cut the cold butter into ½ Tbsp. pats. Prepare the zest of ½ small lemon (or orange) and chop finely. Chop the rosemary into very fine pieces. Add the butter, chopped jalapeños, pecans, rosemary, and lemon zest to a food processor. Process for 5–8 seconds and scrape the bowl. Repeat 2–3 times until a paste has formed. Do not over-process. Spread the pesto over the cooked salmon. **SERVES 4.**

By Keith Tindall from White Egret Farm. Used by permission.

FILLET OF SOLE WITH GREEN GRAPES

1 lb. sole or flounder fillets	¾ cup white wine
Celtic sea salt	¼ lb. seedless green grapes
1 Tbsp. lime juice	1 ½ Tbsp. butter
1 tsp. parsley, finely minced	1 Tbsp. whole-grain flour (soaked)
½ tsp. tarragon, finely minced	2 Tbsp. orange juice
½ clove garlic, minced	

Rinse the fillets and pat dry. Sprinkle fillets with salt and lime juice. Place in a lightly greased skillet. Sprinkle the fillets with the parsley, tarragon, and garlic. Add the wine and simmer for 12 to 15 minutes until the fish flake easily and look milky white but not transparent. Add the grapes the last 5 minutes. Remove fish from the heat and keep warm on a platter. In the original skillet, melt the butter with the remaining juices. Blend in the flour until smooth. Add the orange juice and cook, stirring until the mixture thickens. Add more wine to adjust the consistency. Pour this sauce over the fillets. **SERVES 3–4.**

By Keith Tindall from White Egret Farm. Used by permission.

RED SNAPPER MEXICAN STYLE

4 red snapper fillets	1 bunch cilantro, chopped
2 Tbsp. lime juice	1 tsp. fresh chili pepper, diced
Extra-virgin olive oil	2 cloves garlic, peeled and mashed
1 medium onion, thinly sliced	Pinch of cinnamon
2 ripe tomatoes, peeled, seeded, and chopped	Sea salt

Rub fillets with lime juice; let stand, covered, in refrigerator for several hours.

Using a heavy skillet, sauté the fillets in a little olive oil briefly, on both sides. Transfer to an oiled Pyrex baking dish. Add more olive oil to the skillet. Sauté onion until soft. Add remaining ingredients and simmer for about 30 minutes or more until most of liquid is absorbed. Season to taste with sea salt. Strew the sauce over fish and bake at 350 degrees until tender, about 25 minutes. **SERVES 4.**

From *Nourishing Traditions* by Sally Fallon. Used by permission.

TUNA STEAKS, ORIENTAL STYLE

2 lb. tuna steak, about 1 inch thick	1 Tbsp. raw, unheated honey
Extra-virgin olive oil	½ cup rice vinegar
Sea salt and freshly ground pepper	2 Tbsp. fish sauce (optional)
3 cloves garlic, peeled	1 Tbsp. toasted sesame oil
¼ cup fresh ginger, peeled and coarsely chopped	⅓ cup extra-virgin coconut oil
	1 bunch green onions, chopped
2 Tbsp. Dijon-type mustard	3 Tbsp. sesame seeds, toasted in oven
¼ cup soy sauce	

Brush tuna steaks with coconut oil and sprinkle with salt and pepper. Grill about 5 minutes per side on a barbecue or under a broiler. Transfer to a heated platter and keep warm until ready to serve. Meanwhile, place garlic, ginger, mustard, fish sauce, and soy sauce in food processor; process until blended. Add honey and vinegar and process again. With motor running, add oil gradually so that sauce emulsifies and becomes thick.

Place tuna steak servings on warmed plates. Spoon sauce over and garnish with green onions and sesame seeds. This dish goes well with spinach, chard, Chinese peas, or steamed Chinese cabbage. **SERVES 6.**

From *Nourishing Traditions* by Sally Fallon. Used by permission. For more tuna recipes, order a copy of *Nourishing Traditions*. (See Appendix B in *The Maker's Diet*.)

TUNA SALAD

1 can water-packed tuna	Chopped onions
1 Tbsp. omega-3 mayonnaise	Chopped peppers
1 Tbsp. flaxseed oil or garlic-chili flax	Chopped celery

Combine all ingredients and serve over lettuce or on toasted sprouted bread. **SERVES 1–2.**

By Jordan Rubin

Fowl

CHICKEN SALAD

6 oz. chopped chicken	• Chopped onions
1 Tbsp. omega-3 mayonnaise	• Chopped peppers
1 Tbsp. flaxseed oil or garlic-chili flax	• Chopped celery

Combine all ingredients and serve over lettuce or on toasted sprouted bread. **SERVES 1–2.**

By Jordan Rubin

CHICKEN WITH OREGANO AND MUSHROOMS

1 broiler, cut in pieces (pasture fed)	• 1 clove garlic, minced
¼ cup olive oil	• 2 tomatoes, peeled and quartered
½ cup onion, chopped	• ½ cup dry white wine
1 tsp. salt	• 8 oz. fresh mushrooms, sliced
⅛ tsp. pepper	• ¼ cup parsley, chopped for garnish
¼ tsp. oregano, dried, or ½ tsp. fresh oregano, finely chopped	

Brown the chicken pieces slowly in hot olive oil. Add onion, and cook until soft. Drain the oil, and season chicken with salt and pepper. Add oregano, garlic, wine, and mushrooms. Scrape the bottom of the pan to loosen browned bits. Cover and cook over low heat until the chicken is tender, about 35 minutes. Add tomatoes. Continue cooking for 5 more minutes. Garnish with parsley. **SERVES 4.**

By Keith Tindall from White Egret Farm. Used by permission.

CILANTRO LIME CHICKEN CACCIATORE

2 lb. chicken breast sliced into 1-oz. cubes	2 Tbsp. extra-virgin olive oil
1 Tbsp. minced garlic	5 medium-sized Roma tomatoes
½ cup freshly squeezed lime juice	Celtic sea salt to taste
3 Tbsp. chopped cilantro	Cayenne pepper to taste

Heat sauté pan to medium. Add olive oil, garlic, cilantro, and ¼ cup of lime juice. Simmer for 4–6 minutes. While simmering, pour ¼ cup of lime juice over chicken; let stand for 1–2 minutes. Season chicken with salt and cayenne pepper. After 4–6 minutes, add seasoned chicken to the pan and cook for 8–10 minutes over medium to medium-high heat. **SERVES 4.**

By Jason Dewberry. Used by permission.

EASY CURRIED CHICKEN

2 cups diced cooked chicken	1 Tbsp. curry powder
2 cups coconut milk/cream	1 tsp. chopped onion
4 Tbsp. butter	½ cup lemon juice
3 Tbsp. whole-grain flour (soaked)	Sea salt and pepper to taste

Melt butter, then add flour and curry powder; cook for 5 minutes. Pour in coconut milk/cream and stir well until boiling. Add the onion, then put in the chicken seasonings and heat. Add lemon juice when ready to serve. Goes great with brown rice and vegetables. **SERVES 6.**

From *The Lazy Person's Whole Food Cookbook* by Stephen Byrnes. Used by permission. For more chicken recipes, order a copy of this cookbook (www.powerhealth.net).

CHICKEN FAJITAS

2 lb. chicken breast cut into strips, about ¼ to ½ inch thick	• 1 green pepper, seeded and cut into julienne strips
6 Tbsp. extra-virgin olive oil	• 2 medium onions, thinly sliced
½ cup lemon or lime juice	• Extra-virgin olive oil
¼ cup pineapple juice (optional)	• 12 sprouted whole-wheat tortillas
4 garlic cloves, peeled and mashed	• Melted butter
½ tsp. chili powder	• Crème fraiche or sour cream for garnish
1 tsp. dried oregano	• Chismole for garnish
½ tsp. dried thyme	• Guacamole for garnish
1 red pepper, seeded and cut into julienne strips	

Make a mixture of oil, lemon or lime juice, pineapple juice, and spices; mix well with the meat. Marinate for several hours. Remove with a slotted spoon to paper towels and pat dry. Using a heavy skillet, sauté the meat, a batch at a time, in olive oil, transferring to a heated platter and keeping warm in the oven. Meanwhile, mix vegetables in marinade. Sauté vegetables in batches in olive oil and strew over meat. Heat tortillas briefly in a heavy cast-iron skillet and brush with melted butter. Serve meat mixture with tortillas and garnishes. **SERVES 4–6.**

From *Nourishing Traditions* by Sally Fallon. Used by permission. For more chicken recipes, order a copy of this cookbook.

SPICY CHICKEN STUFFED PEPPERS

2 free-range chicken breasts	• ½ cup sharp cheddar cheese, shredded
2 Tbsp. stick of butter	• 2–4 red or yellow bell peppers (either whole or halves)
1 cup organic brown rice	
½ cup diced jalapeños (optional)	• 1 slice sprouted or sourdough whole-grain bread
2 cups or cans organic black beans	
2 Tbsp. soy sauce	

Bake chicken breasts at 450 degrees for 30 minutes. After 15 minutes of cooking, baste with butter. Bring 2½ cups of water and 1 cup of brown rice to a boil (if brown rice was soaked overnight, add additional water to make approximately 2½ cups). Stir once, and then let simmer for 45 minutes. Add diced jalapeño peppers and shredded cheese to black beans; and cook on low heat. Add soy sauce to bean mixture, stirring occasionally. Take chicken out of oven and slice. Add to the bean mixture and simmer for 15 minutes. Mix brown rice into bean mixture and chicken and mix well. Cut the tops off of the peppers or cut in halves; place desired amount of stuffing into them. Slice the bread and place on top of stuffed peppers. Bake in oven at 450 degrees for 15 minutes. Serve warm. **SERVES 2–4.**

By Sherry Dewberry. Used by permission.

ROASTED PASTURED CHICKEN

1 pastured chicken, whole, 4–5 lb. (a broiler)	• 1 3-inch sprig rosemary
	• Olive oil
1 apple, small	• Celtic sea salt
1 onion, small	• Pepper, freshly ground
1 stalk celery, plus leaves	

Rinse and drain the chicken. If you are starting with a frozen chicken, be certain it is completely thawed. Preheat the oven to 350 degrees. Quarter and core the apple. Peel and quarter onion. Slice celery into 2- to 3-inch pieces. Add about 2 Tbsp. olive oil to the cavity of the bird. Stuff bird with apple, celery, onion, and rosemary. Rub the outside of the bird with olive oil. Sprinkle bird with salt and freshly ground pepper, and rub them into the skin. Place chicken in a baking dish with 2" sides. Bake approximately 1½ hours or until a meat thermometer reads 180 degrees when pushed into the thigh. Remove the chicken from the oven and allow to rest for approximately 20 minutes before carving. The rest period allows the juices to redistribute and results in more tender meat. **SERVES 4.**

By Keith Tindall from White Egret Farm. Used by permission.

WILD DUCK

4–6 ducks, preferably wild, or 2 domestic ducks may be used	• 4–6 sprigs of celery leaves
	• 4–6 pats of extra-virgin coconut butter
1 small onion	• 1–2 cups dry wine, such as a
1 apple, small to medium in size	• Chardonnay

Preheat the oven to 325 degrees. Rinse and drain the ducks. Quarter the apple and onion and cut each quarter into thirds. Place one pat of butter into the cavity of each duck. Add a sprig of celery leaves, and then one or two of the apple and onion slices to fill the cavity. Place the stuffed duck breast down on a large piece of foil (the size of a cookie sheet for a small wild duck). Fold the foil to make a tight packet, leaving one end open. Add ¼ to ½ cup wine to the packet, depending on the size of the duck. Close the packet. Place each packet in the Dutch oven (breast down). Cover with the lid and place into the preheated oven. The ducks should bake for 2–3 hours depending on size. DO NOT open the lid or the packets until done. The ducks are done when they feel soft. The ducks must steam inside the packets in an airtight pan to become tender. Opening the lid or the packets will allow the steam to escape. For ideal results, ducks must bake long and slow under relatively low heat. **SERVES 4.**

By Keith Tindall from White Egret Farm. Used by permission.

Red Meat and Game

ALL-DAY BEEF STEW

3 lb. beef stew, cut into 1-inch pieces	Several sprigs fresh thyme, tied together
1 cup red wine	2 cloves garlic, peeled and crushed
3–4 cups beef stock	2–3 small pieces orange peel
4 tomatoes, peeled, seeded, and chopped (or 1 can tomatoes)	8 small red potatoes
2 Tbsp. tomato puree	1 pound carrots, peeled and cut into sticks
½ tsp. black peppercorns	Celtic sea salt and freshly ground pepper

This recipe is ideal for working mothers. The ingredients can be assembled in about 15 minutes in the morning—or even the night before. Marinate meat in red wine overnight. (This step is optional.) Place all ingredients except potatoes and carrots in an oven-proof casserole and cook at 250 degrees for 12 hours. Add carrots and potatoes during the last hour. Season to taste. **SERVES 6–8.**

From *Nourishing Traditions* by Sally Fallon. Used by permission.

CHEVON MEAT LOAF

1 lb. ground chevon (goat, preferably grass fed)	2 eggs
1 lb. ground beef (preferably grass fed)	1 tsp. ground thyme
½ onion, finely chopped	¼ tsp. Celtic sea salt
1 small green pepper, finely chopped	⅛ tsp. black pepper
⅔ cup bread crumbs (from sprouted or sour dough whole-grain bread)	1 cup tomato ketchup

Preheat oven to 325 degrees. Add all the ingredients to a large bowl. Mix with your hands until all the ingredients are thoroughly combined. The mixture should feel slightly sticky. Add the mixture to a baking pan with 2-inch sides, and form it into a loaf. Make an indentation longitudinally along the top of the loaf. Fill this with additional tomato ketchup. Bake at 325 degrees for approximately 1¼ hours until the loaf appears slightly brown on top. Test for doneness by checking for an internal temperature of 160 degrees. Allow the loaf to rest before slicing in order to avoid crumbling. **SERVES 4–6.**

By Keith Tindall from White Egret Farm. Used by permission.

EASY BROILED STEAK

1 sirloin or porterhouse steak	Butter

Broil steak under hot flame or in hot frying pan, turning frequently, until well browned. Place on serving dish and season as you like. You may add a pat of butter on top of the steak before serving. **SERVES 1.**

From *The Lazy Person's Whole Food Cookbook* by Stephen Byrnes. Used by permission.

EASY LAMB STEW

1½ lb. lamb stew meat	1½ cups diced potatoes
1½ cups diced carrots	¼ cup chopped onion
1 cup diced celery	1 tsp. Celtic sea salt
¼ cup canned tomatoes	

Brown the lamb in extra-virgin coconut oil. Cover with water and add salt. Simmer until meat is tender. Add vegetables and cover. Simmer for 30 minutes or until vegetables are cooked.

This recipe can be made in a Crock-Pot and left to cook for the whole day. Simply add all your ingredients to the pot, cover, and switch on. **SERVES 6.**

From *The Lazy Person's Whole Food Cookbook* by Stephen Byrnes. Used by permission.

LAMB CHOPS

8 lamb chops	½ cup dry red wine
Freshly ground pepper	2 to 3 cups beef or lamb stock

You will need a very well-seasoned cast-iron skillet for this recipe. Season the lamb chops with pepper and cut off any excess fat. Place the skillet over a moderately high fire. When it is hot, set four chops in the pan. (No fat is required. The lamb chops will render their own fat, enough to keep the chops from sticking.) Cook about 5 minutes until they are rare or medium rare. Keep in a warm oven while you are cooking the second batch and preparing the sauce.

Pour the grease out of the pan and deglaze with the red wine and the beef stock. Boil rapidly, skimming off any dirty foam that rises to the top. Reduce to about ¾ cup. The sauce should be consistency of maple syrup.

Place the lamb chops on heated plates, with their accompanying vegetables, and spoon on the sauce. **SERVES 4.**

From *Nourishing Traditions* by Sally Fallon. Used by permission.

LEG OF LAMB OR CHEVON

1 6–8 lb. leg of lamb or chevon (goat), pasture fed preferred	1 clove garlic, slivered
½ cup Dijon mustard	1-inch piece of ginger, skinned and minced
1 Tbsp. rosemary, fresh and finely minced	2 Tbsp. olive oil

Preheat the oven to 350 degrees. Blend mustard, soy sauce, herbs, and ginger in a bowl. Beat in oil to make a creamy mixture. Make 4 shallow slashes in the meat with a sharp knife; tuck a sliver of garlic into each. Brush the lamb or goat liberally with the sauce and let stand for 1–2 hours. Roast on a rack for 1 ¼ to 1 ½ hours, or until a meat thermometer reads 150 degrees. This will produce a medium degree of doneness. Allow to rest before carving. The temperature will climb to about 160 degrees as the meat rests. **SERVES 4–6.**

By Keith Tindall from White Egret Farm. Used by permission.

EASY PEPPER STEAK

4 equal-sized pieces of steak (sirloin or top round), about 1 inch thick	1 large red onion, chopped into 4 slices
1 egg, beaten and diluted with a little water	Olive oil
	Sea salt and pepper to taste
1 red or yellow pepper, seeded and chopped into 4 slices	Soy sauce

Place steak in a large bowl and add the egg. Sprinkle with salt and pepper and let sit for 15 minutes. Match up the onion and pepper slices. In a shallow baking pan, place enough olive oil to cover the bottom. Place the four steaks in the pan and sprinkle a little soy sauce on top of each. Then place one onion and pepper slice on each. Place under the broiler for 3–4 minutes. When you turn the steaks, be sure to replace the pepper and onion slices back on the tops of the steaks. Cook for another 3–4 minutes. **SERVES 4.**

From *The Lazy Person's Whole Food Cookbook* by Stephen Byrnes. Used by permission.

SIMPLE BEEF BURGUNDY

2 lb. lean beef stew meat in small cubes (preferably from pasture-fed beef)	1 cup burgundy wine
	1 medium onion, chopped
2 Tbsp. whole-grain flour (soaked overnight)	2 carrots, sliced
	8 oz. Crimini mushrooms, sliced
2 Tbsp. butter	1 clove garlic, minced
1 Tbsp. olive oil	1 bay leaf
1 tsp. sea salt or Herbamare	¼ tsp. ground thyme
¼ tsp. pepper	1 Tbsp. parsley, snipped
2 cups brown beef stock (page 37)	

Toss the meat in the flour, salt, and pepper in a brown paper bag. Remove. Brown in the butter/olive oil combination. Add the beef stock, wine, mushrooms, onion, carrots, garlic, bay leaf, and thyme. Simmer 2½ to 3 hours, until the meat is tender. Turn the burner off and add the parsley to the hot mixture. If more liquid is needed during cooking, add more stock and wine in proportions of 2 parts stock to 1 part wine. **SERVES 4–6.**

By Keith Tindall from White Egret Farm. Used by permission.

FAMILY ROAST BEEF

4–5 lb. chuck roast, preferably from grass-fed beef	½ cup Worcestershire sauce
¼ pound butter	Celtic sea salt
	Black pepper, freshly ground

Preheat oven to 325 degrees. Rub the roast with salt and pepper and place in a baking dish with 2-inch sides. In a saucepan, melt the butter and add an equal volume of Worcestershire sauce. Pour the sauce over the roast. Bake slowly at 325 degrees until a meat thermometer reads 150–155 degrees (for medium). Remove the roast from the oven and allow it to rest and redistribute the juices before carving. The temperature will climb to 160 degrees. It is particularly important that grass-fed beef be cooked more slowly at a lower temperature than commercial beef. Grass-fed beef should also be allowed to "coast in" to the desired level of doneness by removing it from the oven several minutes before you think it is done. This preserves the juiciness and produces meat that is tenderer.

NOTE: Worcestershire sauce was originally based on lacto-fermented green English walnut catsup (in addition to the fish pastes).

By Keith Tindall from White Egret Farm. Used by permission.

FRENCH-STYLE LONDON BROIL

1 or 2 flank steaks (preferably from pasture-fed beef)	2 Tbsp. onion, minced
	1 clove garlic, minced
½ cup olive oil	1½ tsp. salt
½ cup burgundy wine	5 drops of Tabasco sauce

Score both sides of the steaks in a diamond pattern about ⅛ inch deep. Combine all the ingredients in a large shallow baking dish. Coat the steaks with the marinade and turn four times during a 2-hour period of marinating in the refrigerator. (You may also marinate overnight.) Remove the steaks from the marinade and broil for 3–5 minutes on each side. To serve, cut diagonally into thin slices. **SERVES 3–4.**

By Keith Tindall from White Egret Farm. Used by permission.

KOREAN BEEF

1 flank steak	6 cloves garlic, peeled and mashed
½ cup soy sauce	2 Tbsp. sesame seeds
2 Tbsp. toasted sesame oil	¼ tsp. cayenne pepper
1 bunch green onions, finely chopped	

Using a very sharp and heavy knife, slice the flank steak as thinly as possible across the grain and on the diagonal. (This will be easier if the meat is partially frozen.) Mix other ingredients and marinate beef in the mixture, refrigerated, for several hours or overnight.

Fold or "ribbon" the strips and stick them on skewers, making 4 to 6 brochettes. Cook on barbecue or under grill, about 5 to 7 minutes per side. Meat should still be rare or medium rare inside. This is delicious with any fermented vegetables, especially ginger carrots. The lactic-acid-producing bacteria in the fermented vegetables are the perfect antidote to carcinogens that may have formed in the meat, especially if it has been barbecued. **SERVES 4.**

From *Nourishing Traditions* by Sally Fallon. Used by permission.

VENISON STEAKS WITH MARINADE

4–6 venison steaks, ½ inch thick	3 or 4 juniper berries
1 Tbsp. butter	1 sprig parsley
2 Tbsp. sesame oil	1 sprig thyme
	2 bay leaves
MARINADE:	1–2 cloves garlic, crushed
1 cup red wine	1 pinch of nutmeg
¼ cup lemon juice	1 tsp. sea salt or Herbamare
½ cup olive oil	1 dash hot pepper sauce

Combine the ingredients in the marinade. Marinate the steaks for 24 hours in the refrigerator. To keep the steaks juicy on the inside but brown on the outside, sauté 5–6 minutes on a side in the butter/sesame oil combination. **SERVES 4–6.**

By Keith Tindall from White Egret Farm. Used by permission.

Organ Meats

Preparation Tip: Try to marinate organ meats for about 2 hours prior to cooking as it will significantly improve the taste. Place meat in container, cover with water, and then add 1–2 Tbsp. of fresh lemon juice, plain yogurt, or raw apple cider vinegar. Cover and place in refrigerator. When ready to cook, pour off water and rinse meat under cold water.

LIVER WITH TURKEY BACON AND ONIONS

1–2 lb. organic beef liver	• 1 egg, beaten
8 pieces of turkey bacon	• ½ cup whole-grain flour (soaked
1 onion, chopped	• overnight)

Marinate the liver before cooking. Wash and dry the liver slices and set aside on a plate. Fry the bacon till crisp in a large skillet or frying pan. Remove bacon from the pan. Dredge the liver slices first in the egg, then in the flour. Place in a skillet and cook in extra-virgin coconut oil or butter.

The pieces will cook quickly, so be sure to turn after 2–3 minutes. (Don't overcook liver; it tastes terrible.) Melt some butter in another skillet and sauté onions in it. Strew the onions over the liver on a large platter and top with crumbled turkey bacon. **SERVES 4–6.**

Note: You can prepare this recipe without the turkey bacon, sautéing the liver in butter or extra-virgin coconut oil instead and serve with onions only.

From *The Lazy Person's Whole Food Cookbook* by Stephen Byrnes. Used by permission.

LIVER, RICE CASSEROLE

1 lb. chopped cooked liver	1 cup boiling water
3 Tbsp. melted butter	1 onion, chopped and sautéed in butter
2 cups cooked brown rice	Herbamare seasoning to taste
2 cups chopped tomatoes (you may use canned)	

Grease your casserole dish. Place onions on the bottom, then liver, then the rice. Add tomatoes, water, and seasoning. Bake at 400 degrees for 20 minutes. **SERVES 6.**

From *The Lazy Person's Whole Food Cookbook* by Stephen Byrnes. Used by permission.

Grains, Nuts, Seeds, and Legumes

PREPARATION TIPS

FOR WHOLE GRAINS: For millet, brown rice, oatmeal, amaranth, etc., soak desired amount of grain in an equal amount of water to which you've added 1 Tbsp. raw vinegar, fresh lemon juice, or plain yogurt. (Use 2–3 Tbsp. if you're cooking a large amount of grain.) Cover and let sit at room temperature for at least 7 hours, preferably longer. When ready to cook, add remaining required amount of water or stock and cook. NOTE: To soak whole-grain flours or pancake mixes, follow the same procedure as above but make sure the flour is mixed well with the soaking water.

FOR RAW BEANS AND LENTILS: Soak desired amount of beans in an equal amount of water to which you've added 1 Tbsp. raw vinegar, fresh lemon juice, or plain yogurt. (Use 2–3 Tbsp. if you're cooking a large amount of beans or lentils.) Cover and let sit at room temperature for at least 7 hours, preferably longer. When ready to cook, discard soaking water; add remaining required amount of water or stock and cook.

FOR RAW NUTS AND SEEDS: Place raw nuts or seeds in a bowl, add 1 Tbsp. sea salt, and cover with water. Leave at room temperature for 6–8 hours. Drain the water. Place nuts on a cookie sheet and dry on low heat in the oven. You can also air-dry the nuts on a towel, but it takes much longer to dry them this way.

SPROUTED ALMONDS

Sprouted almonds are much more digestible than untreated ones. Rinse 3 times per day. Ready in 3 days. A sprout is merely a tiny white appendage, about $\frac{1}{8}$-inch long.

From *Nourishing Traditions* by Sally Fallon. Used by permission.

BREAKFAST PORRIDGE

1 cup oats, steel cut or rolled, or coarsely ground in your own grinder	½ tsp. Celtic sea salt
1 cup water plus 2 Tbsp. fermented whey, yogurt, or buttermilk	1 cup water
	1 Tbsp. flaxseeds (optional)

For highest benefits and best assimilation, porridge should be soaked overnight or even longer. (Ancient recipes from Wales and Brittany called for a 24-hour soaking.) Once soaked, oatmeal cooks up in less than 5 minutes—truly a fast food.

Mix oats and salt with water mixture; cover and let stand at room temperature for at least 7 hours and as long as 24 hours. Bring additional 1 cup of water to boil. Add soaked oats. Reduce heat, cover, and simmer several minutes. Meanwhile, grind flaxseeds in a mini-grinder. Off heat, stir in flaxseeds and let stand for a few minutes. Serve with butter or cream thinned with a little water, and a natural sweetener like Sucanat, date sugar, maple syrup, or raw honey. **SERVES 4.**

From *Nourishing Traditions* by Sally Fallon. Used by permission.

CRISPY PECANS

4 cups pecan halves	Filtered water
1 tsp. sea salt or Herbamare	

The buttery flavor of pecans is enhanced by soaking and slow-oven drying. Soak pecans in salt and filtered water for at least 7 hours or overnight. Drain in a colander. Spread pecans on two stainless steel baking pans and place in a warm oven (no more than 150 degrees) for 12 to 24 hours, stirring occasionally, until completely dry and crisp. Store in an airtight container. Great for school lunches. **MAKES 4 CUPS.**

VARIATION: TAMARI PECANS

In place of salt, add ¼ cup tamari sauce to soaking water.

From *Nourishing Traditions* by Sally Fallon. Used by permission.

EASY BROWN RICE

2 cups brown rice	1 Tbsp. apple cider vinegar or yogurt
4 cups water or 2 cups water mixed with 2 cups chicken stock	

Soak rice in 2 cups of water with the vinegar or yogurt for at least 7 hours. Transfer to your pot or rice cooker. Add the remaining water or water/broth, and cook till tender. If you're cooking the rice on a stovetop, bring to a boil then lower heat to a simmer and cook covered, stirring occasionally. **SERVES 6–8.**

NOTE: This recipe can be used for ANY whole grain you wish to serve by itself—millet, quinoa, buckwheat, amaranth, etc.

From *The Lazy Person's Whole Food Cookbook* by Stephen Byrnes. Used by permission.

EASY FRENCH TOAST

1 cup plain yogurt	½ tsp. sea salt
½ tsp. honey	8 slices sprouted or sourdough whole-grain bread
2 eggs, slightly beaten	

Combine eggs, yogurt, honey, and salt in a mixing bowl. Dip each slice of bread quickly into the mixture. Brown in extra-virgin coconut oil. Serve with butter and unheated honey or maple syrup or fresh fruit. **SERVES 4.**

From *The Lazy Person's Whole Food Cookbook* by Stephen Byrnes. Used by permission.

EASY WHOLE-GRAIN WAFFLES

1⅓ cups whole-grain flour (spelt, kamut)	1 cup water
	2 Tbsp. plain yogurt
¾ tsp. sea salt	4 Tbsp. extra-virgin coconut oil
2 tsp. non-aluminum baking powder	2 eggs, separated
2 Tbsp. unheated honey	

Soak the flour in water with 2 Tbsp. yogurt for at least 7 hours. Separate the eggs. Beat the yolks and add the yogurt and butter. Combine salt, honey, and flour; add

this to the first mixture. Beat the egg whites until they form stiff peaks; fold them into the mix. Mix in the baking powder quickly. Cook in your waffle iron. **Serves 6.**
From *The Lazy Person's Whole Food Cookbook* by Stephen Byrnes. Used by permission.

FIVE-GRAIN CEREAL MIX

2 cups wheat or spelt	2 cups barley or oats
2 cups millet	2 cups split peas or lentils
2 cups short-grain rice	

This combination of grains conforms to the five grains recommended in the *Yellow Emperor's Classic of Internal Medicine*. Mix together and grind coarsely. Store in refrigerator. **Makes 10 cups.**
From *Nourishing Traditions* by Sally Fallon. Used by permission.

FIVE-GRAIN PORRIDGE

1 cup Five-Grain Cereal	½ tsp. Celtic sea salt
1 cup water plus 2 Tbsp. fermented whey or yogurt	1 cup water
	1 Tbsp. flaxseeds (optional)

Mix Five-Grain Cereal and salt with water plus whey or yogurt. Cover and let stand at room temperature for at least 7 hours and as long as 24 hours. Bring additional 1 cup of water to boil. Add soaked cereal. Reduce heat, cover, and simmer several minutes. Meanwhile, grind flaxseed in a mini-grinder. Remove cereal from heat and stir in flaxseed. Serve with butter or cream, thinned with a little water, and a natural sweetener like Sucanat, date sugar, maple syrup, or raw honey. **Serves 4.**
From *Nourishing Traditions* by Sally Fallon. Used by permission.

MUFFINS

1¼ cups freshly ground and/or soaked spelt, kamut, or whole-wheat flour	½ cup extra-virgin coconut oil
¾ cup water mixed with 1 Tbsp. yogurt	⅓ cup honey
1 egg, lightly beaten	2 tsp. baking powder
¼ tsp. fine Celtic sea salt	1 tsp. vanilla

Preheat oven to 400 degrees. Mix flour with water and yogurt and let stand overnight. Mix in remaining ingredients. Pour into well-buttered muffin tin about three-quarters full. Bake for 15–20 minutes. These muffins will puff up and then fall back a bit to form flat tops. Note: 1 cup buckwheat flour or cornmeal may be used in place of 1 cup spelt, kamut, or wheat flour. **Makes about 12.**

Adapted from *Nourishing Traditions* by Sally Fallon. Used by permission.

Variation: RAISIN MUFFINS

Add ½ cup raisins and ½ tsp. cinnamon to batter.

Variation: BLUEBERRY MUFFINS

Pour batter into muffin tins. Place 5–7 blueberries, fresh or frozen, on each muffin. Berries will fall into the muffins. (If they are added to the batter, they sink to the bottom of the muffin.)

Variation: DRIED CHERRY MUFFINS

Add 4 oz. dried cherries (available at health food stores and gourmet markets) and ½ cup chopped crispy pecans to batter.

Variation: FRUIT SPICE MUFFINS

Add 2 ripe pears or peaches, peeled and cut into small pieces, and ½ tsp. cinnamon, ⅛ tsp. cloves, and ⅛ tsp. nutmeg to batter.

Variation: LEMON MUFFINS

Add grated rind of 2 lemons and ½ cup chopped crispy pecans to batter. Omit vanilla.

Variation: GINGER MUFFINS

Add 1 Tbsp. freshly grated ginger and 1 tsp. ground ginger to batter. Omit vanilla.

BLUEBERRY PECAN PANCAKES

1½ cups freshly ground or soaked spelt, kamut, or whole-wheat flour	½ cup crispy pecans
	¼ tsp. fine Celtic sea salt
¾ cup water mixed with 1 Tbsp. yogurt	½ cup extra-virgin coconut oil
1 egg, lightly beaten	2 tsp. baking powder
½ cup blueberries (fresh or frozen)	1 tsp. vanilla

Mix flour with water and yogurt and let stand overnight. Defrost blueberries in refrigerator if frozen. Mix ingredients into a bowl. Heat extra-virgin coconut oil in a skillet or pan over low heat. Increase temperature to moderate heat. Use about 3 Tbsp. of batter for each pancake. Serve with honey, maple syrup, or butter. **MAKES ABOUT 12.**

VARIATIONS: Use different kinds of fruit.

From *Nourishing Traditions* by Sally Fallon. Used by permission.

PEPITAS

4 cups raw, hulled pumpkinseeds	1 tsp. cayenne pepper (optional)
1 Tbsp. sea salt or Herbamare	Filtered water

This recipe imitates Aztec practices of soaking seeds in brine, then letting them dry in the hot sun. They ate pepitas whole or ground into meal.

Dissolve salt in water and add pumpkinseeds and optional cayenne. Soak for at least 7 hours or overnight. Drain in a colander, then spread on 2 stainless steel baking pans. Place in a warm oven (no more than 150 degrees) for about 12 hours or overnight, stirring occasionally, until thoroughly dry and crisp. Store in an airtight container. **MAKES 4 CUPS.**

VARIATION: TAMARI PEPITAS Use 2 Tbsp. tamari sauce in place of sea salt and cayenne.

From *Nourishing Traditions* by Sally Fallon. Used by permission.

SIMPLE BEANS

2 cups black beans, kidney beans, pinto beans, black-eyed beans, or white beans Filtered water	2 Tbsp. whey 1 tsp. sea salt 4 cloves garlic, peeled and mashed (optional)

Soak beans in filtered water, salt, and whey for 12–24 hours, depending on the size of the bean. Drain, rinse, place in a large pot, and add water to cover beans. Bring to a boil, skimming off foam. Reduce heat and add optional garlic. Simmer, covered, for 4–8 hours. Check occasionally and add more water as necessary. **SERVES 8.**

From *Nourishing Traditions* by Sally Fallon. Used by permission.

SIMPLE LENTILS

2 cups lentils, preferably green lentils Filtered water 2 Tbsp. homemade whey or yogurt 1 tsp. Celtic sea salt 2 cups beef or chicken stock	2 cloves garlic, peeled and mashed Several sprigs fresh thyme, tied together 1 tsp. dried peppercorns, crushed Pinch dried chili flakes (optional) Juice of 1–2 lemons

Soak lentils in filtered water, salt, and whey for several hours. Drain and rinse. Place in a pot and add stock to cover. Bring to a boil and skim. Add remaining ingredients except lemon and simmer, uncovered, for about 1 hour, or until liquid has completely reduced. Add lemon juice and season to taste. Serve with a slotted spoon. Excellent with sauerkraut and strongly flavored meats such as duck, game, or lamb. **SERVES 6–8.**

From *Nourishing Traditions* by Sally Fallon. Used by permission.

SPROUTED SUNFLOWER SEEDS

These are among the most satisfactory seeds for sprouting. Sunflower sprouts are just delicious in salads, but they must be eaten very soon after sprouting is accomplished, as they soon go black. Try to find hulled sunflower seeds packed in nitrogen packs. Rinse 2 times per day. Ready in 12 to 18 hours, when sprout is just barely showing.

From *Nourishing Traditions* by Sally Fallon. Used by permission.

Beverages

APPLE "CIDER"

1 gallon unfiltered, unpasteurized apple juice 1 Tbsp. sea salt	½ cup homemade whey

Place all ingredients in a large bowl. Cover and leave at room temperature for 2 days. Skim foam that rises to the top. Line a strainer with several layers of cheesecloth; strain juice into jars or jugs. Cover tightly and refrigerate. Flavors will develop slowly over several weeks. The "cider" will eventually develop a rich buttery taste.

If you wish to further clarify the cider, add lightly beaten egg whites to the jugs (1 egg white per quart). Set aside a few hours, and then filter again through several layers of cheesecloth. **MAKES 4 QUARTS.**

From *Nourishing Traditions* by Sally Fallon. Used by permission.

BALANCED VEGETABLE JUICE

Vegetable juices can be a great source of essential nutrients. Here is a staple vegetable juice blend:

50 percent carrot juice	1 tsp. cream, goat's milk yogurt, coconut milk
10 percent beet juice	
30 percent celery juice	1–2 Tbsp. of Green Superfood Powder with HSOs (optional)
10 percent parsley or other green juice	

By Jordan Rubin

CULTURED VEGETABLE JUICE

3 red beets	1 oz. grated ginger
1 carrot	1 tsp. fine Celtic sea salt
2–4 Tbsp. fermented whey or 1 packet cultured vegetable starter	Purified water

Peel and chop beets and carrot; combine with peeled and grated ginger. Place in a 1–2 quart glass container with a seal. Cover with water and add whey and salt. Stir well and cover. Leave at room temperature for 2–3 days, then transfer to the refrigerator.

By Jordan Rubin

GINGER ALE

¾ cup ginger, peeled and finely chopped or grated	2 tsp. Celtic sea salt
½ cup fresh lime juice	¼ cup homemade whey
¼–½ cup Rapadura or dehydrated cane juice	2 quarts filtered water

Place all ingredients in a 2-quart jug and fill with water. Stir well and cover tightly. Keep at room temperature for two days before transferring to the refrigerator. This will keep several months well chilled. To serve, strain and mix half ginger ale with half purified water or naturally sparkling water. Best consumed at room temperature, not cold. **MAKES 2 QUARTS.**

From *Nourishing Traditions* by Sally Fallon. Used by permission.

HOMEMADE KEFIR

1 qt. raw goat's or cow's milk	1 packet kefir starter

Pour into quart-size Mason jar. Add kefir starter. Set in a room temperature area for 12–48 hours, then transfer to refrigerator. A cupboard is an ideal place to ferment. The temperature range should be between 70–75 degrees. Kefir can last several months in the refrigerator and will become sourer over time.

By Jordan Rubin

NEW WINE

1 case organic concord, black, or red grapes, about 16 lb.	½ cup Probiogurt or continental acidophilus 1 Tbsp. Celtic sea salt

This beverage is best made with a vegetable juicer, although a high-speed blender or food processor will do. It takes a bit of time, but the results are worth it. This delicious and refreshing drink is an excellent substitute for wine, containing all the nutrients of grapes found in wine, including many enzymes, but none of the alcohol. In fact, a drink similar to this may have been what the Bible referred to as "new wine."

Remove grapes from stems, wash well, and pass through the juicer. Place liquid in a large bowl with salt and Probiogurt, and stir well. Cover and leave at room temperature for 2 days. If you don't use a juicer, you may want to scoop off the skins and strain juice through a strainer lined with several layers of cheesecloth. It is best to store new wine in airtight containers in refrigerator. Delicious flavors will develop over time. May be served diluted with half water. **MAKES 5–6 QUARTS.**

By Jordan Rubin

RASPBERRY DRINK

2 12-oz. packages frozen raspberries, or
24 oz. fresh raspberries
Juice of 12 oranges
¼–½ cup Rapadura or dehydrated
cane juice

¼ cup homemade whey
2 tsp. Celtic sea salt
2 quarts filtered water

Place raspberries in food processor and blend until smooth. Mix in a large bowl with remaining ingredients. Cover and let sit at room temperature for 2 days. Skim foam that may rise to top. Strain through a strainer lined with cheesecloth. Pour into jugs or jars. Cover tightly and store in refrigerator. If you wish to further clarify the raspberry drink, add lightly beaten egg whites to the jugs (1 egg white per quart). Set aside a few hours, and then filter again through several layers of cheesecloth. To serve, dilute with sparkling mineral water. **MAKES 2 QUARTS.**

From *Nourishing Traditions* by Sally Fallon. Used by permission.

Smoothies

Author's note: During my healing process, I consumed this smoothie one to two times per day with raw eggs. Contrary to popular belief, eggs from healthy, free-range, pastured chickens are almost always free of dangerous germs. If the egg has an odor, obviously it should not be eaten. Since most of the salmonella infections are caused by germs on the shell, for added protection it is best to wash the eggs in the shell with a mild alcohol or hydrogen peroxide solution or a fruit and vegetable wash.

BERRY SMOOTHIE

10 oz. plain whole-milk yogurt, kefir, or coconut milk/cream	1 Tbsp. flaxseed or hempseed oil
	1–2 Tbsp. unheated honey
1–2 raw high omega-3 whole eggs (optional)	1 Tbsp. goat's milk protein powder (optional)
1 Tbsp. extra-virgin coconut oil	1–2 cups fresh or frozen berries

Combine ingredients in a high-speed blender.

Properly prepared, this smoothie is an extraordinary source of easy-to-absorb nutrition. It contains large amounts of "live" enzymes, probiotics, vitally important "live" proteins, and a full spectrum of essential fatty acids. Smoothies should be consumed immediately or refrigerated for up to 24 hours. If frozen in ice cube trays with a toothpick inserted into each cube, smoothies can make for a great frozen dessert. **Makes 2 8-oz. servings.**

By Jordan Rubin

VARIATIONS FOR SMOOTHIES

To enjoy the same life giving nutrients with different flavors, add the following ingredients to the "basic" ingredients used in the smoothie listed above:

BANANA COCONUT CREAM SMOOTHIE—10 oz. coconut milk/ cream (instead of whole-milk yogurt or kefir); 1–2 fresh or frozen bananas (instead of berries); ½ tsp. vanilla extract

BLACKBERRY BANANA SMOOTHIE—½–1 cup fresh or frozen blackberries (instead of berries); 1 fresh or frozen banana

CHERRY VANILLA SMOOTHIE—½–1 cup fresh or frozen cherries (instead of berries); 1 fresh or frozen banana

CHOCOLATE MOUSSE SMOOTHIE—2 Tbsp. cocoa or carob powder or Healthy Chocolate Spread (instead of berries)

CREAMSICLE SMOOTHIE—6 oz. (not 10) of plain whole-milk yogurt or kefir; 4 oz. freshly squeezed orange juice; 1–2 fresh or frozen bananas (instead of berries)

MOCHA SWISS ALMOND SMOOTHIE—2 Tbsp. cocoa or carob powder (instead of berries); 2 Tbsp. raw almond butter (or 4 Tbsp. Chocolate Almond Spread)

MOCHACCINO SMOOTHIE—2 Tbsp. cocoa or carob powder; 1 Tbsp. organic-roasted coffee beans; 1–2 fresh or frozen bananas (instead of berries)

PEACHES 'N CREAM SMOOTHIE—½–1 cup fresh or frozen peaches (instead of berries); 1 fresh or frozen banana

PINA COLADA SMOOTHIE—10 oz. coconut milk/cream (no whole-milk yogurt or kefir); 1 cup fresh or frozen pineapple (instead of berries); 1 fresh or frozen banana

By Jordan Rubin

Snacks and Desserts

BANANA BREAD

3 cups freshly ground spelt or wheat flour
2 cups cultured buttermilk, water mixed with 2 Tbsp. whey or yogurt
3 eggs, lightly beaten
1 tsp. sea salt
¼ to ½ cup maple syrup
2 tsp. baking soda
¼ cup melted butter
2 ripe bananas, mashed
½ cup chopped crispy pecans

Mix flour with buttermilk or water mixture and let stand overnight. Beat in remaining ingredients. Pour into a well-buttered and floured loaf pan. Bake at 350 degrees for 1 hour or more, until a toothpick comes out clean. **MAKES ONE 9 x 13 LOAF.**

For variations of this recipe, order a copy of *Nourishing Traditions* by Sally Fallon. (See Appendix B in *The Maker's Diet.*)

COCONUT ALMOND FUDGE

1 cup extra-virgin coconut oil
¾ cup carob powder
¼ cup raw almond butter
¼ cup unheated honey
1 Tbsp. vanilla

Place all ingredients in a glass container and set in simmering water until melted if needed. Mix together well. Spread thick paste mixture on a piece of buttered parchment paper; allow to cool in refrigerator or freezer. Remove and serve immediately. **MAKES 1¼ CUP.**

By Jordan Rubin

PINEAPPLE CREAMY TREAT

1 cup organic ricotta cheese
1 Tbsp. unheated honey
½ tsp. vanilla extract
1 cup pineapple or fruit of choice

Mix ricotta, honey, and vanilla extract. Top with fruit of choice. **SERVES 2–3.**

By Jordan Rubin

CREAMY HIGH-ENZYME DESSERT

4 oz. Probiogurt, plain yogurt, or cultured cream 1 Tbsp. raw, unheated honey	1 tsp. flaxseed oil ½ cup fresh or frozen organic berries

Mix yogurt, honey, and flaxseed oil. Top with berries.

By Jordan Rubin

SUPER SEED BAR

¾ cup and 3 Tbsp. SuperSeed Whole Food Fiber Powder ½ cup tahini (sesame butter) ½ cup almond butter ¼ cup and 1 Tbsp. Goatein goat's milk protein powder	6 Tbsp. cocoa or carob powder ¼ tsp. salt ⅓ cup honey 2½ Tbsp. extra-virgin coconut oil 1 tsp. vanilla extract 1 tsp. orange or almond extract

Combine wet and dry ingredients and form into bars. Freeze or refrigerate. **MAKES 4–6 3-OZ. BARS.**

By Phyllis Rubin. Used by permission.

VARIATIONS Add organic chocolate or carob chips, shredded coconut, dried fruit, or chopped almonds.

TRAIL MIX

1 cup crispy pecans 1 cup crispy cashews 1 cup unsulphured dried apricots, apples, pears, or pineapple cut into pieces	1 cup raisins 1 cup dried sweetened coconut meat 1 cup carob chips (optional)

Mix all ingredients together. Store in an airtight container. **MAKES 5–6 CUPS.**

From *Nourishing Traditions* by Sally Fallon. Used by permission.

ZESTY POPCORN

⅓ cup popcorn	2 Tbsp. melted butter
3 Tbsp. extra-virgin coconut oil	Herbamare to taste
2 Tbsp. garlic-chili flax	

Melt coconut oil in pan over medium heat. Pour popcorn into pan. Cover pan with lid. While popping, melt butter. Cook until popped. Pour into large bowl. Pour melted butter and garlic chili-flax and seasoning and mix thoroughly.

By Nicki Rubin. Used by permission.

Section 3

Shopping Lists

AS YOU HAVE SEEN, THE MAKER'S DIET 40-DAY HEALTH Experience is organized around three phases. Phase one puts you back on the path toward eating well. Once you have learned the principles of healthy eating, phase two adds in more foods to enjoy. Phase three adds even more foods, and is the maintenance phase for going beyond the fortieth day in the health the Creator designed.

The shopping lists given here reflect the allowed foods lists from *The Maker's Diet* and are listed according to the three phases of the program. Take these to the grocery store and shop with confidence. To shop for individual recipes, you'll want to reference the recipe itself for specific ingredients.

Phase One

As with virtually any important task or endeavor, *the way you start* significantly affects the results you enjoy at the finish. Phase one of the Maker's Diet is designed to stabilize insulin and blood sugar, reduce inflammation, reduce infection, enhance digestion, and help balance the hormones in your body. This should help you better manage your weight in a healthy manner and significantly improve your overall health.

Best of all, the components of phase one should greatly reduce your risk of incurring disease. It effectively helps your body reduce insulin sensitivity and balance the omega-3/omega-6 ratio that is so vital to balance levels of inflammation and enhance the health of your immune system, which will reduce chances of infection.

Temporary Food Limitations

After reading through this forty-day program, you will notice that phase one restricts disaccharide-rich carbohydrate foods such as grains, pastas, breads, sugar, potatoes, corn, beans, and legumes. While it is true that the people of the Bible consumed a diet that contained liberal amounts of grain and other carbohydrate foods, they were higher-quality, lesser-processed carbohydrates, and therefore much easier to digest. And since they ate smaller quantities of food (some believe as much as six times less food than we do), their typical diet was close to a modern lower-carbohydrate diet.

Also, these people would have eaten extremely healthy diets since birth, so they weren't hampered by increased insulin sensitivity, endocrine imbalances (including thyroid problems), infection, inflammation, and digestive problems common to people who have been reared with the standard American diet (SAD). Since phase one is designed to *correct* these harmful imbalances, it must *temporarily* limit even healthy foods such as fruits, whole grains, and honey while allowing for the liberal consumption of protein foods, vegetables, and healthy oils.

Phase One Shopping List

Meat (grass-fed/organic is best)

- Beef
- Veal
- Lamb
- Buffalo
- Venison
- Elk
- Goat
- Meat bone soup/stock
- Liver and heart (must be organic)
- Beef or buffalo sausage or hot dogs (no pork casing—organic and nitrite/nitrate free is best) (Use sparingly in phase one.)

Fish (wild freshwater/ocean-caught fish is best; make sure it has fins and scales!)

- Salmon
- Halibut
- Tuna
- Cod
- Scrod
- Grouper
- Haddock
- Mahi mahi
- Pompano
- Wahoo
- Trout
- Tilapia
- Orange roughy
- Sea bass
- Snapper
- Mackerel
- Herring
- Sole
- Whitefish
- Fish bone soup/stock
- Salmon (canned in spring water)
- Tuna (canned in spring water)
- Sardines (canned in water or olive oil only)

Poultry (pastured/organic is best)

- Chicken
- Cornish game hen
- Guinea fowl
- Turkey
- Poultry bone soup/stock
- Duck

- Chicken or turkey bacon (no pork casing—organic and nitrite/nitrate free is best)
- Chicken or turkey sausage or hot dogs (no pork casing—organic and nitrite/nitrate free is best) (Use sparingly in phase one.)
- Liver and heart (must be organic)

Eggs (high omega-3/DHA is best)
- Chicken eggs (whole with yolk)
- Duck eggs (whole with yolk)

Dairy
- Goat's milk yogurt (plain)
- Homemade kefir from goat's milk
- Soft goat's milk cheese
- Goat's milk hard cheese
- Sheep's milk hard cheeses

Fats and oils (organic is best)
- Oil, butter (ghee)
- Avocado
- Goat's milk butter
- Cow's milk butter, organic
- Extra-virgin coconut oil (best for cooking)
- Extra-virgin olive oil (not best for cooking)
- Flaxseed oil (not for cooking)
- Hempseed oil (not for cooking)
- Goat's milk butter (not for cooking)
- Raw cow's milk butter, grass-fed (not for cooking)
- Expeller-pressed sesame oil
- Coconut milk/cream (canned)

Vegetables (organic fresh or frozen is best)
- Squash (winter or summer)
- Broccoli

- Asparagus
- Cauliflower
- Cabbage
- Celery
- Eggplant
- Garlic
- Lettuce (leaf of all kinds)
- Spinach
- Peas
- String beans
- Beets
- Brussels sprouts
- Carrots
- Cucumber
- Pumpkin
- Onion
- Okra
- Mushrooms
- Peppers
- Tomatoes
- Artichoke (French, not Jerusalem)
- Leafy greens (kale, collard, broccoli rabe, mustard greens, etc.)
- Raw leafy greens (endive, escarole, radicchio, arugula, frisse, etc.)
- Sprouts (broccoli, sunflower, pea shoots, radish, etc.)
- Sea vegetables (kelp, dulse, nori, kombu, hijiki)
- Raw, fermented vegetables (lacto-fermented only, no vinegar)

Beans and legumes (soaked or fermented is best)
- Small amounts of fermented soybean paste (miso) as a broth
- Lentils

Nuts and seeds (organic, raw, or soaked is best)
- Almonds (raw)
- Hempseed (raw)

- Sunflower seeds (raw)
- Hempseed butter (raw)
- Pumpkinseed butter (raw)
- Pumpkinseeds (raw)
- Flaxseed (raw and ground)
- Almond butter (raw)
- Sunflower butter (raw)
- Tahini, sesame butter (raw)

Condiments, spices, seasonings (organic is best)

- Salsa (fresh or canned)
- Tomato sauce (no added sugar)
- Guacamole (fresh)
- Apple cider vinegar
- Celtic sea salt
- Mustard
- Herbamare seasoning
- Omega-3 mayonnaise
- Umeboshi paste
- Soy sauce (wheat free), tamari
- Raw salad dressings and marinades (see recipes)
- Herbs and spices (no added stabilizers)
- Pickled ginger (preservative and color free)
- Wasabe (preservative and color free)
- Organic flavoring extracts (alcohol based, no sugar added), i.e., vanilla, almond, etc.

Fruits (organic fresh or frozen is best)

- Blueberries
- Strawberries
- Blackberries
- Raspberries
- Cherries
- Grapefruit
- Lemon
- Lime

Beverages

- Purified, nonchlorinated water
- Natural sparkling water, no carbonation added (i.e., Perrier)
- Herbal teas (preferably organic)—unsweetened or with a small amount of honey or Stevia
- Raw vegetable juice (beet or carrot juice—maximum 25 percent of total)
- Lacto-fermented beverages (see recipes)
- Certified organic coffee—buy whole beans, freeze them, and grind yourself when desired; flavor only with organic cream and a small amount of honey.

Sweeteners

- Unheated, raw honey in very small amounts (1 Tbsp. per day maximum)

Miscellaneous

- Goat's milk protein powder

Phase Two

Congratulations on finishing phase one. It was a tough two weeks, but I trust it was well worth it. No doubt you are feeling much better. If you started out overweight, you may be as many as 10 pounds lighter. Your digestion has improved, your energy levels have increased, your skin looks better, and you are well on your road to optimal health. Phase two introduces a greater variety of foods, including seeds and fruit.

Phase Two Shopping List

Meat (grass-fed/organic is best)
- All meats listed in phase one

Fish (wild freshwater/ocean-caught fish is best—check for fins and scales!)
- All fish listed in phase one

Poultry (pastured/organic is best)
- All poultry listed in phase one

Eggs
- Fish roe or caviar (fresh, not preserved)

Luncheon meat (organic and nitrite/nitrate free is best)
- Turkey, sliced (free range, preservative free)
- Roast beef, sliced (free range, preservative free)

Dairy (organic, grass-fed is best)
- Homemade kefir from raw or nonhomogenized cow's milk
- Kefir from pasteurized, nonhomogenized cow's milk
- Raw cow's milk hard cheeses
- Cow's milk cottage cheeses
- Cow's milk ricotta cheese
- Cow's milk plain whole-milk yogurt
- Cow's milk plain kefir
- Cow's milk plain sour cream
- Raw goat's milk

Fats and oils (organic is best)
- Expeller-pressed peanut oil

Vegetables (organic fresh or frozen is best)
- Sweet potatoes
- Corn
- Yams

Beans and legumes (soaked or fermented is best)
- White beans
- Kidney beans
- Tempeh (fermented soybean)
- Black beans
- Navy beans

Nuts and seeds (organic, raw, soaked is best)
- Walnuts (raw)
- Hazelnuts (raw)
- Pecans (raw or soaked and low-temperature dehydrated)
- Macadamia nuts (raw)
- Brazil nuts (raw)

Condiments, spices, seasonings (organic is best)

- Ketchup (no sugar)
- All-natural salad dressings (no preservatives)
- All-natural marinades (no preservatives)

Fruits (organic fresh or frozen is best)

- Apples
- Grapes
- Peaches
- Pears
- Kiwi
- Pomegranates
- Guava
- Apricots
- Melon
- Oranges
- Plums
- Pineapple
- Passion fruit

Beverages

- Raw vegetable juice (beet or carrot—maximum 50 percent of total)
- Coconut water

Sweeteners

- Unheated raw honey (up to 3 tablespoons per day)
- Stevia

Miscellaneous

- Same as phase one

Phase Three

Phase three should begin in the fifth week of the program or when you are feeling a renewed sense of health and are approaching your ideal weight. Phase three is the maintenance phase of the diet. This allows consumption of foods from each food group. Here we will introduce healthy grain foods and foods higher in sugars and starches, such as sweet potatoes.

Phase Three Shopping List

Meat (grass-fed/organic is best)
• All meats listed in phase one and phase two

Fish (wild freshwater/ocean-caught fish is best—check for fins and scales!)
• All fish listed in phase one and phase two

Poultry (pastured/organic is best)
• All poultry listed in phase one and phase two

Eggs (high omega-3/DHA or organic is best)
• All eggs listed in phase one and phase two

Luncheon meat (organic is best)
• All luncheon meat listed in phase two

Dairy
• All dairy listed in phase one and phase two

Fats and oils (organic is best)
• All fats and oils listed in phase one and phase two

Vegetables (organic fresh or frozen is best)
• All vegetables listed in phase one and phase two

Beans and legumes (soaked or fermented is best)

Along with beans and legumes listed in phase one and phase two, add:

- Pinto beans
- Red beans
- Split peas
- Garbanzo beans
- Lima beans
- Broad beans
- Black-eyed peas
- Edamame (boiled soybeans) (in small amounts)

Nuts and seeds (organic, raw, soaked is best)

Along with nuts and seeds listed in phase one and phase two, add:

- Almonds (dry roasted)
- Walnuts (dry roasted)
- Almond butter (roasted)
- Tahini (roasted)
- Pecans (dry roasted)
- Macadamia nuts (dry roasted)
- Sunflower seeds (dry roasted)
- Pumpkinseeds (dry roasted)
- Pumpkinseed butter (roasted)
- Sunflower butter (roasted)
- Peanuts, dry roasted (must be organic) (in small quantities)
- Peanut butter, roasted (must be organic) (in small quantities)
- Cashews, raw or dry roasted (in small quantities)
- Cashew butter, raw or roasted (in small quantities)

Condiments, spices, seasonings (organic is best)

- All condiments, spices, and seasonings listed in phase one and phase two

Fruits (organic fresh or frozen is best)

Along with fruits listed in phase one and phase two, add:

- Banana
- Mango

- Papaya
- Canned fruit (in its own juices)
- Dried fruit (no sugar or sulfites): raisins, figs, dates, prunes, pineapple, papaya, peaches, and apples

Beverages

Along with beverages listed in phase one and phase two, add:
- Raw, unpasteurized vegetable juice
- Raw, unpasteurized fruit juice
- Organic wine and beer (in very small amounts)

Grains and starchy carbohydrates (whole-grain, organic, soaked is best)
- Sprouted, Ezekiel-type bread
- Sprouted Essene bread
- Fermented whole-grain sourdough bread
- Quinoa
- Amaranth
- Buckwheat
- Millet
- Spelt (in small quantities)
- Sprouted cereal
- Whole-grain kamut or spelt pasta (in small quantities)
- Oats (in small quantities)
- Kamut (in small quantities)
- Brown rice (in small quantities)
- Barley (in small quantities)

Sweeteners

Along with sweeteners listed in phase one and phase two, add:
- Maple syrup

Miscellaneous
- Selected healthy snacks (a few times per week) (See Appendix B in *The Maker's Diet*.)
- Trail Mix (page 87)

- Organic chocolate spreads
- Carob powder
- Zesty Popcorn (page 88)

Conclusion

THE MAKER'S DIET SHOPPER'S GUIDE SHOULD STAY AT your fingertips through the forty days of the Maker's Diet 40-Day Health Experience. It gives you daily help in the places you and your family need it most: the kitchen, the dinner table, and the grocery store. This is where we live, and this is where the victory for total wellness is won.

Then when the forty-first day comes, you will still want to keep *The Maker's Diet Shopper's Guide* close at hand. The shopping lists, recipes, and meal plans will be great resources for you as you live a life of health according to *The Maker's Diet*.

Made in the USA
Middletown, DE
29 December 2019

82167193R00066